the human operating system

an owner's manual

"You cannot teach a man anything; you can only help him discover it within himself."

Galileo

senn delaney
the culture-shaping firm

HEIDRICK & STRUGGLES

Fifth Edition 2011.
Copyright © 1994-2017 by Senn Delaney Leadership Consulting
Group, LLC. All Rights Reserved. Fifth Edition 2011.

No part of this book may be reproduced in any form without
permission in writing from the publishers. Senn Delaney Leadership Consulting
Group, LLC.

Library of Congress Catalog Card Number: 94077892
Senn, Larry E.
1. Leadership. 2. Teambuilding. 3. Culture Shaping.
4. Management. 5. Managing Change. 6. Empowerment.
7. Personal Effectiveness. 8. Relationships. 9. Business.
I. Senn, Larry, E. II. Title.

Designed by: Paul R. Diniakos, Senn Delaney
Fifth edition cover and page design by: Paul R. Diniakos, Senn Delaney

Fifteenth Printing, Fifth Edition 2011

Printing number
15   16   17   18   19   20   21   22   23   24   25

For more information, please contact:
Senn Delaney
7755 Center Avenue, Suite 900
Huntington Beach, CA 92647
t (800) 788-3380
f (562) 426-5174

senn delaney
the culture-shaping firm

HEIDRICK & STRUGGLES

© 1994-2017 Senn Delaney Leadership Consulting Group, LLC. All rights reserved.

table of contents

© 1994-2017 Senn Delaney Leadership Consulting Group, LLC. All rights reserved

senn delaney
the culture-shaping firm

HEIDRICK & STRUGGLES

how to use this book to get the most value

This book has been written to help you deepen your understanding of the concepts from your unfreezing session and apply them to contribute to your organization's culture-shaping efforts. It will do so by leading you through many simple, common-sense principles that are fundamental to healthy, high-performance teams and cultures.

Since culture change begins at the individual level—it all starts with you.

The concepts presented in the book are principles of leadership as well as life effectiveness. They are presented in an interactive way to help you understand them in terms of your everyday life. In this book, you can learn how to improve your quality of life. You will also learn how to manage change, be a better coach, feel more empowered, get more results in less time, work with and influence others, and shape a culture.

Each chapter closes with questions, action steps and/or assignments to help you increase your own effectiveness and contribute to healthy team dynamics, and to help your organization achieve better results. For instance, at the end of chapter four (Behavioral Styles), you can complete a behavioral-styles questionnaire to learn more about how you relate to others. Chapter twelve (Blue-Chip Mindset) contains tips and questions to help you identify and focus on the blue-chip priorities in your work life as well as your personal life.

We suggest that you read the following material in short segments, taking time to reflect on how it applies to your own situation. You will probably want to read the segments that are most meaningful to you many times over. You will find that your understanding deepens with each reading.

You can approach this book in a variety of ways:

- Read it as you would any instructive book to expand your knowledge and skills.
- Read it in the weeks after your unfreezing session to relive your experience and learn ways to apply the concepts day-to-day.
- Use it as a reference book to learn more about selected topics you feel would assist you or your team to better support your organization's culture-shaping efforts.
- Read a chapter with a teammate and then discuss and coach one another.
- Suggest that your team read a selected chapter and then meet to discuss applications and team agreements.

In this era of competing priorities, many organizations neglect one of their most important investments—the growth and development of people. Your organization has made a wise choice by investing in you. We invite you to invest in yourself by taking the time to read this book. We know you will appreciate the dividends.

HEIDRICK & STRUGGLES

© 1994-2017 Senn Delaney Leadership Consulting Group, LLC. All rights reserved.

1

the human operating system

high performance—three levels: individual, team and organization

This book and the Senn Delaney culture-shaping process are designed to help you, your team and your organization create more success with less stress. It provides benefits at three levels:

For you as an individual—Leadership and life effectiveness

For your team—High-performance team dynamics

For your organization—Creation of a winning culture

These levels are interrelated. High-performance teams working together toward common goals create a winning culture. In such a culture, people are accountable, respectful, collaborative and resilient.

We have received a great deal of feedback over the years from people who have participated in our culture-shaping process. They tell us that, when applied, the concepts we present result in very real and meaningful benefits in their lives and careers. The changes they report include:

- Greater results and added satisfaction in life
- More success with less stress
- Better balance
- Improved relationships
- Greater resilience to change
- Better influencing skills
- Added leadership and life effectiveness
- Healthier, better-performing teams and cultures

senn delaney
the culture-shaping firm

HEIDRICK & STRUGGLES

© 1994-2017 Senn Delaney Leadership Consulting Group, LLC. All rights reserved.

the human operating system

There are a number of underlying principles to the Senn Delaney culture-shaping methodology. Possibly the most important is an understanding of what we call the Human Operating System. When the CEO of one of the largest computer firms in the world participated in this process, he observed that the reason computers around the world can work together efficiently is that they share a common operating system. He went on to say, "We now have a common understanding of a 'Human Operating System' that allows us to interact in more productive and healthier ways."

Many of the experiences in the unfreezing session you attended were designed to give you real-time insights into the Human Operating System so that you can learn to deal with people and events more effectively. As you may recall, early on the first day, we conduct a rapid "handshake mill." The purpose of that exercise is to give people an experience that instantly changes (raises) the level of energy in the room. This experience also introduces the first principle of the Human Operating System.

> 1.   Energy: Managing personal energy is a key to healthy, high performance.

While human energy is subjective, it also is very powerful. Sometimes we feel we have plenty of energy to do what we need to do; other times, we feel short of energy both at work and afterwards, when we arrive home. There are certain people around us that seem to increase our energy, while others seem to drain it. We all have been on teams where energy was absent, or very negative, and results were poor and/or extremely stressful. We have also experienced teams with lots of positive, creative energy where results flowed easily.

Positive energy isn't always the high or "hyper" energy, like in the handshake mill. While we need bursts of that occasionally, too much would eventually wear us out. We can also be very resourceful and productive with a much calmer, more reflective, creative energy. In a like manner, negative, non-productive energy can also be high and low. Worry and depression are examples of lower negative energy; anger and self-righteousness are examples of high negative energy.

In these very demanding times, at work and in life, we each need to be more aware of this first principle regarding energy. A noted leadership expert who deals with both athletes and executives contends that managing personal energy is more important than managing time. To do that, we each need to find ways to better create and direct positive energy in ourselves and in those we influence.

We can't begin to do that if we don't notice it. Since energy is a feeling, one tool we have to help notice our feelings is the Mood Elevator.

senn delaney
the culture-shaping firm

HEIDRICK & STRUGGLES   © 1994-2017 Senn Delaney Leadership Consulting Group, LLC. All rights reserved.

up the mood elevator

Learning to identify the quality of our thinking has a lot to do with something most of us see as unwanted distractions in our lives—our moods. Remember the Mood Elevator from the session. It is tied to the next principle of the Human Operating System:

2. Moods
   Our state of mind (moods) determines:
   - Our effectiveness
   - Our quality of life

Most of us think of our moods as obstacles, things that get in the way of our effectiveness. In reality, moods are one of the most important tools we have in achieving results. The Mood Elevator is a barometer of the quality of our thinking. Higher-quality thinking creates higher mood feelings. Lower-quality thinking creates low mood states.

"Fair warning, I'm in one of my 'moods'."

www.cartoonbank.com

Have you ever been cruising along, having a nice day, when suddenly everything seemed to go downhill? Conversely, have you ever been dealing with tough, complex issues and yet you felt confident and resourceful?

Just as our thoughts fluctuate from moment to moment, so does the quality of our thinking. At the times when we are at our best, we tend to feel optimistic and confident. We see the best in others and in ourselves. During times like these, we would say that we are experiencing higher-quality thinking. At those times, our behavior is usually more effective. Things seem to work out better for us.

We've all experienced times like this. We may not even be aware that we are thinking; it seems like answers come to us from "out of the blue" and we are amazed at our own brilliance. Athletes refer to these times as "being in the zone"; when everything just seems to go right without a lot of effort.

Of course, we also experience times when we feel frustrated, confused, impatient or angry. We tend to see the worst in others. When we feel like this, we are experiencing lower-quality thinking. Our behavior at these times is usually less than effective—we often feel like our own worst enemy.

Have you ever tried to give feedback or coach someone when you were irritated or angry? How well did it go?

© 1994-2017 Senn Delaney Leadership Consulting Group, LLC. All rights reserved.

HEIDRICK & STRUGGLES

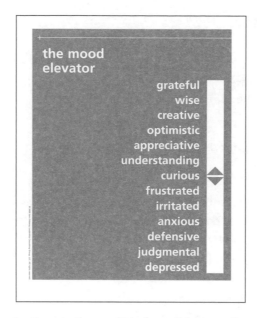

the mood elevator

grateful
wise
creative
optimistic
appreciative
understanding
curious
frustrated
irritated
anxious
defensive
judgmental
depressed

The moment-to-moment fluctuations in the quality of our thinking affect the way we feel, or our moods. The Mood Elevator is a tool we can use to notice when our thinking is "off," or unreliable. When experiencing higher-quality thinking, we have feelings at the higher end of the elevator, such as gratitude, generosity, creativity, insight, appreciation, compassion and understanding. When we are experiencing lower-quality thinking, we have feelings like impatience, frustration, hostility, anxiety and judgment. Using our moods to gauge the quality of our thinking helps us to know when our thinking is reliable and when it is not, so we can make decisions with greater perspective and avoid being driven by lower-quality thoughts or thought habits.

Higher-quality thinking gives us greater "emotional intelligence." If we can learn to identify the quality of our thinking, we will begin to make better choices, exhibit more effective behaviors more often, and avoid less-than-effective behaviors.

For example, one of the most useful levels in the Mood Elevator is "curious." If someone does something we don't understand, we often become irritated and judgmental. How much more effective could we be if we directed our energy to being curious: "I wonder why they see it that way?" This type of shift can actually change the quality of our relationships and our lives.

Naturally, the fact that we are all human means we all ride up and down the Mood Elevator. We cannot always be at the top of our game, nor will we always be at the bottom. We may visit a level like "judgmental" or "frustrated," but if we accept that this is all part of the human condition and surrender to the fact that sometimes we feel good and sometimes we don't, we will eventually move back up the Mood Elevator. Unfortunately, you've probably met people who, without even being aware of it, seem to have permanently set up shop on these levels.

Being aware of these connections can help us avoid being "trapped" at the bottom of the Mood Elevator, and is the first step in being able to positively impact behavior and get better results. We will explore this concept further in chapter three, entitled "At Your Best."

what drives our behaviors and moods? the results cone

Why do we behave the way we do? Where do our moods come from? We can answer this through a model we call the Results Cone. This model demonstrates the relationship between our thinking and our results.

senn delaney
the culture-shaping firm

HEIDRICK & STRUGGLES

© 1994-2017 Senn Delaney Leadership Consulting Group, LLC. All rights reserved.

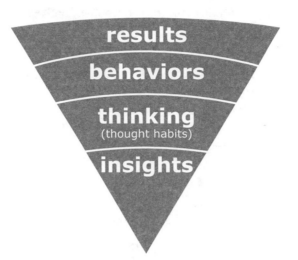

The results we achieve are the outcome of our behaviors. So where does our behavior come from? What lies behind the tangible behavior is something not so tangible: our thinking or, more accurately, the **thought habits** we've developed throughout our lives. In the session, the arm-wrestle game is an example of how many people have the thought habit, "For me to win, someone else has to lose."

The third principle of the Human Operating System is:

3. Power of thought:
    - Our thinking drives our behaviors.
    - Our thoughts determine our moods and our moment-to-moment experience of life.

As human beings, we are constantly thinking. Most of the time, we are not aware of the exact nature of our thoughts or even that we are thinking! Yet our entire experience of life is determined by our moment-to-moment thinking and unique thought habits. Our thinking also drives our moods: Worried thinking creates worried feelings; hopeful thinking creates hopeful feelings. These thoughts, thought habits and feelings are continually driving our behavior and ultimately, our results. It works something like this:

Thought Habit: "In order for me to win, someone else has to lose."

Behaviors: Unhealthy competition within a company or team; people are unwilling to share information or resources.

Results: Time and energy is wasted on defensive maneuvering, having to "re-invent the wheel" because information is not shared. Productivity decreases; costs increase.

If, however, my thinking is, "We're all in this together," then I am more likely to look for ways to win as a whole team, and will achieve better results both personally and for my organization.

Thought Habit: "If I can't say something nice, then I shouldn't say anything at all."

Behaviors: People are reluctant to coach others or offer valuable developmental feedback.

Results: People unknowingly waste time and resources on less-than-effective pursuits. Productivity, profitability and teamwork suffer.

© 1994 2017 Senn Delaney Leadership Consulting Group, LLC. All rights reserved.

If, on the other hand, I believe that giving constructive feedback and appreciation is an important part of developing my team, I'll do it easily and consistently, thereby improving the productivity of my team and ultimately the profitability of my organization.

Most people are not aware of the connection between their thinking and their results. Thought habits are an unconscious pattern, because our thinking is usually invisible to us. The first step in increasing our personal effectiveness is to become aware of some of our more pervasive thought habits and consider how they might drive our behavior—and ultimately our results. The Senn Delaney process gives you insights into your habits so you can make new choices. We call it "insight-based learning."

CALVIN AND HOBBES; ©1991 Watterson Reprinted with permission of Universal Press Syndicate. All rights reserved.

thought habits at work

Energy, moods, quality of thinking and culture are all very subjective yet powerful notions. Recognizing and spending time on these things has not always been acceptable in business. When Senn Delaney began its work with organizational culture in the 1970s, we were entering largely uncharted territory. Most business leaders at that time did not place much importance on dealing with the subjective side of business, and culture was not a word in the business vocabulary. In the early 80s, Tom Peters, then a consultant with McKinsey and Company, gathered data on the power of the subjective for the book *In Search of Excellence*, co-written with Robert Waterman.[1] Peters and Waterman determined that the subjective factors of business, such as style of management, interpersonal skills and shared values, or culture, were critical elements for organizational success. However, as a rule, people still tend to neglect these factors.

In Search of Excellence was based on a McKinsey and Company organization analysis model called "The 7-S Model."

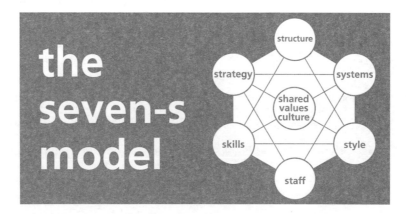

HEIDRICK & STRUGGLES   © 1994-2017 Senn Delaney Leadership Consulting Group, LLC. All rights reserved.

The model analyzed successful and unsuccessful organizations by looking at seven variables. There were three "hard" or objective S's—strategy, structure and systems; and four "soft" or subjective S's—skills, staff, style and shared values/culture. The authors identified key cultural qualities of the successful organizations as things like "bias for action" and "close to the customer."

The research found that, of the organizations studied, the most successful were more skilled at working on both sets of S's. The less-successful organizations tended to ignore, discount or neglect the "soft" side. Of all of the subjective S's, shared values/culture turned out to be the most significant factor in success.

The Human Operating System helps to illustrate why we tend to neglect the powerful subjective side.

filters

The fourth and final principle of the Human Operating System is:

4. Blind spots and selective perception:
    Life events, situations and people look different to each of us because we each have:
    ■ Selective perception
    ■ Blind spots
    ■ Our own unique memory and filters
    (Caution: Things are not as they appear)

Earlier in this chapter, we discussed how each of us experiences the world differently. Another way to describe this is that each of us sees the world through a unique set of filters. Our filters cause each one of us to see things differently from anyone else—they "color" our experience of life.

We all have filters that take different forms. The following list is not all-inclusive by any means, but typical filters that tend to operate for all of us include our:

■ Past experiences

■ Values

■ Beliefs/thought habits

■ State of mind or moods

■ Behavioral style

■ Gender/age

■ Race/religion

These filters, combined with our moment-to-moment thought process, create what is called our selective perception.

selective perception

Since it is impossible to be aware of everything that is happening at any one time, we are "selectively" aware. What we focus on in any given situation is shaped by our filters and thought processes. In the session, when we looked at the collage with dozens of items, each person focused on a different set of objects. Another example of this is what happens when we start to shop for a new car. Suddenly we begin to see the same model everywhere we go! Of course, we realize that they have always been there, but we didn't notice them before.

© 1994-2017 Senn Delaney Leadership Consulting Group, LLC. All rights reserved.   HEIDRICK & STRUGGLES

Once we selectively perceive any situation, we have a tendency to assume that what we see is the whole picture—we think that this is what others see, or should see, as well. That tendency is at the core of many conflicts we experience throughout our lives. It is further compounded because once we see things a given way, it becomes very difficult to see another point of view. We call this "lock-in/lock-out." This phenomenon can cause serious relationship issues and leadership disputes. We can at times become very inflexible when we believe that our perception is the "truth" and others are wrong, when in fact we just see things differently. To the extent that we can understand this, we can be more respectful of other points of view and our relationships and results will improve.

The image below can help illustrate how the phenomenon of selective perception works. What do you see?

Figure 9.4 M.C. Escher's "Circle Limit IV" © 2006 The M.C. Escher Company-Holland. All rights reserved.

Most people initially see either bats (black) or angels (white). Which did you see first? If you saw the angels first, it probably took some effort to see the bats—or vice versa. We also have a tendency to do this in our lives.

Here's an example:

During a department meeting, one manager remarked that he was ready to implement a change and was confident he had identified and dealt with all possible obstacles.

When a direct report attempted to offer several alternate ideas, the manager's first reaction was "that would be a waste of time." Upon further reflection, he decided to ask for more input from the direct report. To his surprise, he found that his direct report had seen a number of things he had missed that were ultimately critical to the success of the change.

The direct report had simply looked at it from a different point of view.

We must become aware that selective perception and the lock-in/lock-out phenomenon can cause people to react to things differently. When people don't behave the same way we do, we all have a tendency to assume that it's due to some defect in the other person's personality. Relationships would be much smoother if we could understand that people aren't "defective"; they just see the world as a slightly different place than we do.

senn delaney
the culture-shaping firm

HEIDRICK & STRUGGLES

© 1994-2017 Senn Delaney Leadership Consulting Group, LLC. All rights reserved.

How often have you been caught up in a discussion believing you are right, only to find out later that there was more to the story than you realized? Being aware of the concept of selective perception can make a real difference in results and relationships.

"I never realized they had feelings."

© The New Yorker Collection 1989 Warren Miller from cartoonbank.com. All Rights Reserved.

blind spots

The key to better understanding and dealing with the subjective dimension of business is to help us become more aware of the blind spots each of us has, due in part to our intellectual "wiring." Understanding how our brain functions can help us to become better leaders, teammates and performers.

Our brain is divided into two hemispheres:

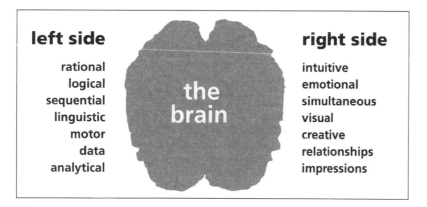

left side	**the brain**	**right side**
rational		intuitive
logical		emotional
sequential		simultaneous
linguistic		visual
motor		creative
data		relationships
analytical		impressions

The two hemispheres of our brain control completely different functions. As you'll note in the graphic above, the left side controls our objective (tangible or "hard") side and the right side controls our subjective (intangible or "soft") side.

Neuroanotomist Jill Bolte Taylor, Ph.D. was a scientist at Harvard when she had a profound first-hand experience of the disparate functions of the right and left cranial hemispheres: at the age of 37, she had a massive stroke when a blood vessel exploded in the left side of her brain. As this was occurring, she observed her left-brain functions completely shut down in the span of four hours. Yet, amazingly, her working right brain provided her with a total sense of well-being and even euphoria.

© 1994-2017 Senn Delaney Leadership Consulting Group, LLC. All rights reserved.

senn delaney
the culture-shaping firm

HEIDRICK & STRUGGLES

In her book, *My Stroke of Insight*, she describes how this experience helped her understand the differences in the brain hemispheres. "My right hemisphere is all about right here, right now," she says. "My right mind is all about the richness of this present moment. It is filled with gratitude for my life and everyone and everything in it. It is content, compassionate, nurturing, and eternally optimistic. To my right mind character, there is no judgment of good/bad or right/wrong, so everything exists on a continuum of relativity."[2]

Alternatively, the left hemisphere "is one if the finest tools in the universe when it comes to organizing information. My left hemisphere personality takes pride in its ability to categorize, organize, describe, judge, and critically analyze absolutely everything," Taylor writes. "To keep up with life's experiences in the external world, my left mind processes information remarkably fast—much faster than my right hemisphere."[3]

Because of its speed and organizational ability, most of us have grown up learning to use our left brain much more often than our right—through elementary school learning the 3R's, and through high school learning algebra, science or a second language. For many of us, our first job required us to quickly learn a number of new skills and tasks, and so again, we focused on using our left brain.

As we move into management positions where relationships, influencing people and innovation are important, we can run into trouble. The problem is that our right brain, which helps us do things like lead and develop people, and to think creatively, is under-developed.

Fortunately, as Taylor learned throughout her eight-year recovery process, we have the ability to recalibrate our brain's circuitry. She says of human brain cells: "Thanks to their neural plasticity, their ability to shift and change their connections with other cells, you and I walk the earth with the ability to be flexible in our thinking, adaptable to our environment, and capable of choosing who and how we want to be in this world. Fortunately, how we choose to be today is not predetermined by how we were yesterday."[4]

The world we live in is far too complex to think with only half a brain! To be at our best in this day and age, we need take Taylor's advice and learn to use both sides of our brain well.

The F's exercise from the session also makes this point very well. Here is another version of that exercise for you to try:

How many F's do you see when you quickly look at the sentence below?

> Finished files are the result of
>
> years of scientific study combined
>
> with the experience of years.

Do you think you got them all? After experiencing the exercise, you were more aware of your blind spots, so you probably did better this time. (See the answer on the next page.)

senn delaney
the culture-shaping firm

HEIDRICK & STRUGGLES

© 1994-2017 Senn Delaney Leadership Consulting Group, LLC. All rights reserved.

"That, at any rate, is the situation as my coolly analytical left brain sees it. Now let me communicate, if I can, my right brain's gut reaction."

Drawing by J. Handelsman; ©1986 Harvard Business Review.

Because we have spent so much time developing the left side of our brain, whenever we are put to a task, we tend to overuse the left brain and override the right. This can be useful when we have to analyze data, but it can also create serious blind spots, much as you saw in the above exercise where most people came up short in counting the F's. The left side of our brain tends to discount the "ofs" buried in the sentences, either because it sees them as inconsequential words, or because the linguistic (sound) function of the brain "sees" the word "of" as "ov." **(By the way, there were 6 F's this time.)**

So remember:

- Things are not always as they appear. Be willing to entertain the notion that you may not have the whole picture.

- When someone sees things differently, try to understand their point of view; they might know something you don't.

- Get input from multiple sources so they can help point out possible "blind spots."

summary

One of the premises of our process is that every person sees the world differently because the way we view things is determined by our own thinking in any given moment. Getting better results and creating more success with less stress requires an understanding of the Human Operating System, or the subjective aspect of the human experience.

1. **Energy:** Managing personal energy is a key to healthy, high performance.

2. **Moods:** Our state of mind (moods) determines:

   - Our effectiveness.

   - Our quality of life.

3. Power of thought:
   - Our thinking drives our behaviors.
   - Our thoughts determine our moods and our moment-to-moment experience of life.

4. **Blind spots and selective perception:** Life events, situations and people look different to each of us because we each have:

   - Selective perception

   - Blind spots

   - Our own unique memory and filters

© 1994-2017 Senn Delaney Leadership Consulting Group, LLC. All rights reserved.

HEIDRICK & STRUGGLES

questions, action steps and assignments

1. Reflect on several projects you are working on. Where might some of your blind spots be? How might you be able to use the wisdom of your team to help ensure you see the whole picture?

    _____

    _____

    _____

    _____

    _____

2. Reflect on the last several weeks. When were you in a high-quality thinking state? When were you in a low-quality thinking state? What were your familiar feelings like in each instance?

    High:

    _____

    _____

    _____

    _____

    Low:

    _____

    _____

    _____

    _____

3. Can you see a connection between your moods and your effectiveness? Describe that connection in your own words.

    _____

    _____

    _____

    _____

    _____

    _____

    _____

senn delaney
the culture-shaping firm

HEIDRICK & STRUGGLES

© 1994-2017 Senn Delaney Leadership Consulting Group, LLC. All rights reserved.

2

be here now

"He who lives in the present lives in eternity."

Ludwig Wittgenstein

- Sarah finished describing the complicated situation and asked, "What do you think? Should we go forward?" Her supervisor blinked and said, "What? ... I'm sorry, what did you say?"

- Although the budget meeting started right on time—the director of marketing was standing in the doorway giving last minute instructions to an assistant; the head of information services was reviewing a new printout; the sales manager was talking on a cellular phone to an important client; and two other department heads were discussing a problem with the head of communications.

- Sam made it to his son's little league game at the last minute but his head was still full of the crisis at work. On the way home Tommy gushed non-stop about the game, then suddenly stopped and wailed, "Dad, you are not listening!"

It happens every day—two people have a conversation but one of them is not really there; a meeting is held but participants are concerned about other issues; a person goes home but leaves his or her mind at the office. When people are doing one thing but thinking about another, they are generally not effective at either.

> Have you ever been with someone who was not there?
>
> Have you ever been with someone and you were not there?
>
> Have you ever been at a meeting and no one was there?
>
> Have you ever gone home and left your brain at work?

© 1994-2017 Senn Delaney Leadership Consulting Group, LLC. All rights reserved.

HEIDRICK & STRUGGLES

"Honey, I'm home."

© The New Yorker Collection 1988 Mick Stevens from cartoonbank.com. All Rights Reserved.

Most of us have fallen into the habit of not being present. This chapter will enhance your understanding of this habit and enable you to spend more time in the present for maximum effectiveness.

After learning about the **Be Here Now** concept, one man had a realization that he was actually contributing to the inefficiency of the meetings he was attending. This is how he describes his insight and how it has helped him change that behavior:

> "I had a belief that an effective manager must be able to not just manage but 'do' multiple projects or tasks at the same time. So one habit I picked up was to review my 'in' basket while attending meetings.

> "This had two negative consequences: One, I was not 'there' to contribute effectively at the meeting; and two, people at the meeting felt I did not value their input or contributions since I was not paying full attention to their presentation of ideas or to their discussions. Now, I make a conscientious effort to contribute fully to the team's effort at meetings and I am choosy about which meetings I attend."

We are often so caught up in thinking about the past or the future that we lose our ability to be present in the moment. The consequences of this behavior are very far-reaching:

- We are not as creative as we can be. When we are distracted by thoughts of the past or present, our busy minds prevent us from tapping into our wisdom and common sense, or the more intuitive side of our brain.

- We do not listen well to others so they do not feel heard or respected.

- Our quality of life at home suffers because we cannot turn off the whirlpool of thoughts about work. This affects our relationships with our loved ones and robs our ability to recharge our batteries so we can be more effective when we go back to work.

Being fully present and aware in the moment at hand, without being distracted, is what we call Be Here Now. It provides our greatest opportunities for maximizing effectiveness and life fulfillment.

With our rapidly changing world and the uncertainty that comes with it, the importance of balance, focus and being present is more critical than ever. As people's awareness of this concept increases, their lives often change dramatically. When they begin to quiet their minds just a little, they are not as distracted by worry, judgments, preconceived notions, thinking about too many things at once, self-doubts or insecurity.

HEIDRICK & STRUGGLES

© 1994-2017 Senn Delaney Leadership Consulting Group, LLC. All rights reserved.

One manager from a recent session told us this story about how Be Here Now affected his life:

> "I learned about the importance of Be Here Now a couple of years ago. Although reluctant to give up my valuable weekend time, my wife always managed to convince me that we should routinely visit her parents, especially on special occasions. She would say, 'My parents will not always be around and I want to make sure I spend valuable time with them while they are living.'

> "Through the wisdom of my wife, I realized the importance of this concept. While I was spending time visiting my own mom, I was not Being Here Now. Since that time I have been much better at spending quality time with her. She is a special lady who has sacrificed a lot to make me successful."

the value of be here now

What is the value in Being Here Now?

- **Better balance of personal and professional life:** The more we can be fully present both at home and at work, the more we will have rich, nourishing, fulfilling environments in both places.
- **Easier, more fulfilling relationships:** When people feel heard and appreciated, they feel better about you and about themselves, and are more likely to produce their best efforts.
- **Less stress, more peace of mind:** When we think about the past or worry about the future, our thoughts create stress and diminish our peace of mind. Living in the present moment reduces the anxiety these distractions can bring.
- **Better creativity:** Have you ever noticed that you tend to get your best ideas when you are in a more reflective state and your thinking has slowed down, such as in the shower, or just before you fall asleep at night? That is because a quieter mind, one not full of distracting thoughts, has room to come up with good ideas. The more you can Be Here Now, the more this will happen.
- **Increased productivity and quality:** When we are present and undistracted, we can focus our efforts and reach our highest levels of performance.

listening

The ability to listen fully and openly to another person is a very important benefit of Being Here Now. In fact, one way to get better at Being Here Now is to practice listening. This provides added benefit because listening builds rapport in relationships and provides us with better information to make decisions and solve problems more creatively.

Most people acknowledge that they are not great listeners. Even those that think they are pretty good might get a different answer from loved ones, friends or co-workers. True listening means much more than just hearing the words the person is saying. Former California senator Dr. S.I. Hayakawa defines listening in the following way:

> "Listening does not mean simply maintaining a polite silence while you are rehearsing in your mind the speech you are going to make the next time

© 1994-2017 Senn Delaney Leadership Consulting Group, LLC. All rights reserved.

HEIDRICK & STRUGGLES

you grab a conversational opening. Nor does listening mean waiting alertly for the flaws in the other fellow's arguments so that later you can mow him down. Listening means trying to see the problem the way the speaker sees it, which means not sympathy—which is feeling for him—but empathy, which is experiencing with him. Listening requires entering actively and imaginatively into the other fellow's situation and trying to understand a frame of reference different from your own."[5]

Good listening requires listening to what is being said with an open mind rather than judging whether the person or content of their conversation is right or wrong. Listening with an open mind, when you are undistracted, allows you to step into the other person's shoes and see their point of view—how they see the world. This is what we call listening to understand.

Good listening also allows you to understand what is not being said. It's the ability to listen to more than just the words being spoken. When you're present and listening, you'll find that you notice messages sent through gestures, facial expressions, posture, voice tones, underlying emotions and the speaker's energy. More than half of the message is carried by these non-verbal gestures, and we only notice them when we quiet our minds and listen at a deeper level.

Listening, like other concepts such as the Mood Elevator, has vertical dimensions. The chart below illustrates these.

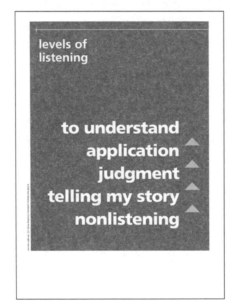

the different levels of listening

The deepest and most effective listening occurs when minds are free of distractions and we are Being Here Now for the other person. The paragraphs below describe the different levels of listening. Which one is a habit for you?

Nonlistening or Listening to Tell My Story

Unfortunately, most of us have been on the receiving end of the lower levels of listening. There are times when the person you're talking to simply isn't listening, or is obviously just waiting for you to take a breath so that they can jump in and tell you their story. Clearly, this type of listening isn't helpful to anyone.

HEIDRICK & STRUGGLES   © 1994-2017 Senn Delaney Leadership Consulting Group, LLC. All rights reserved.

Listening to Judge or Evaluate

At this level, the listener's thinking process is caught up in disagreement or agreement and comparing what is heard to beliefs, past experiences, pre-conceived conclusions or expectations. The listener's thoughts are steeped in memory and the listener cannot Be Here Now. They may have an emotional reaction to, or judgment about, the content of the person's words, rather than being attuned to the message behind the words.

Listening to "How it Applies to Me"

This type of thinking can be characterized as logical and linear. It involves coming up with techniques and solutions in terms of what can be done next. Whenever the listener feels the need to "do something" with what is being said, the more distracted the listener becomes and therefore is less likely to notice the more subtle aspects of the other person's communication.

Listening to Understand

In this state, a person's level of Be Here Now enables them to hear the entire message, understand the other person beyond the words being spoken and gain insight and perspective about the person's state of mind.

Drawing by S. Paro Lini; Reprinted The Saturday Evening Post ©1994

The following poem gives us some additional insights about how to listen and focus on Being Here Now. It is a plea from an unknown author to listen for understanding.

> When I ask you to listen to me and you start giving advice, you have not done what I asked.
>
> When I ask you to listen to me and you begin to tell me why I shouldn't feel that way, you are trampling on my feelings.
>
> When I ask you to listen to me and you feel you have to do something to solve my problem, you have failed me, strange as that may seem.
>
> All I asked was that you listen, not talk or do—just listen to me.
>
> Advice is cheap: 25 cents will get you both Dear Abby and Billy Graham in the same newspaper.
>
> And I can do for myself: I'm not helpless, maybe discouraged and faltering, but not helpless.

senn delaney
the culture-shaping firm

HEIDRICK & STRUGGLES

© 1994-2017 Senn Delaney Leadership Consulting Group, LLC All rights reserved.

When you do something for me that I can and need to do for myself, you contribute to my fear and weakness.

But when you accept as a simple fact that I do feel what I feel, no matter how irrational, then I can quit trying to convince you and can get about the business of understanding what is behind this irrational feeling. And when that is clear, the answers are obvious and I don't need advice. Irrational feelings make sense when we understand what is behind them.

Perhaps that is why prayer works, sometimes, for some people, because God is mute and He doesn't give advice or try to fix things. He just listens and lets you work it out for yourself.

So please listen and just hear me. And, if you want to talk, wait a minute for your turn; and I'll listen to you.

living in the here and now

Though Being Here Now can dramatically improve our ability to listen and communicate, there is much more to Be Here Now—in fact, it can improve every facet of our lives. You may have heard athletes talk about being "in the zone," when their minds quiet down and their bodies achieve their greatest strength, speed or accuracy. People in other fields use similar phrases to explain what occurs. President Harry Truman spoke of quieting his mind and being more creative in his "personal foxhole." Creative people and leaders in many fields speak of getting into the "flow."

Each is speaking of a way of life that invites us to quiet our busy minds, rely on our innate wisdom and creativity, and live each moment of life to the fullest. It is a state in which we are responsive to the moment and not distracted by thoughts about the past, the future, judgment or ego. In this state, our sense of enjoyment and appreciation of almost any situation is very rich. We respond to challenges with greater perspective. We are sensitive to the environment and to people around us, and we are sometimes surprised at how creatively we think in any given situation.

We usually know we've been there only after it happens, for when we are fully in the moment nothing else exists, including reflection on the moment.

Reflect now on times when you have been in that state. What is that like for you?

Clearly, the experience of Being Here Now, is rich, fulfilling and allows us to be much more productive. Most of us would like to spend more time in that state. So how do we do that?

The three keys to living a more fulfilling, productive life are **understanding, awareness and acceptance**. It is important to understand that in Being Here Now, we are not controlled by the situations in which we find ourselves. We can be in the most stressful situations, surrounded by distractions, but as long as we are present in the moment, the quality of our thinking will stay high and intact, allowing us to maintain our bearings and make sensible decisions.

Nor does Being Here Now mean that we are not thinking; we are thinking all the time. What it does mean is that the quality of our thinking is higher. We are insightful, creative, or even brilliant, because our minds are freed of the distractions that pull us out of the present moment. This allows us to get the most out of every moment.

If we were to characterize the distracting thoughts we experience in our lives, they would tend to fall into one of four categories:

HEIDRICK & STRUGGLES   © 1994-2017 Senn Delaney Leadership Consulting Group, LLC. All rights reserved.

- Thoughts, worries or concerns about the future
- Guilt or regret about events in the past
- Ego or image issues about how "I" might be showing up
- Thoughts about how we fit into our surroundings and the environment we live in—our culture, family or origin

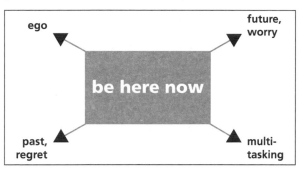

During times of change, we tend to experience the most distraction. All these thoughts tend to take us out of the present and our effectiveness diminishes at a time when we need to be at our best. To the degree we can quiet our minds and minimize these distractions, the quality of our experience and the quality of our effectiveness likewise improves. One way to think about change is as a tornado. Although the tornado itself is an explosive force of swirling energy and chaos, the center of the tornado is always calm and serene. The term used by meteorologists to describe the center of the tornado is "the eye of the storm."

Of course, it is not possible to live a life free of distraction. But the more we can see our thoughts for what they are—just distractions—the better we are able to minimize their power over us.

the mood elevator and be here now

We also have a built-in tool that tells us if we're Being Here Now: our feelings. The feelings we experience on the upper end of the Mood Elevator are indicators of Be Here Now: humor, contentment, compassion and gratitude. Conversely, the feelings we experience on the lower end of the Mood Elevator are indicators of when we are distracted, of not Being Here Now: impatience, defensiveness, judgment, anxiety, and anger.

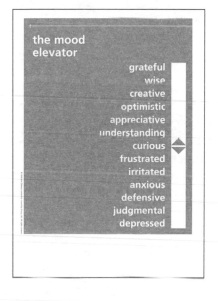

© 1994-2017 Senn Delaney Leadership Consulting Group, LLC All rights reserved.

What are the feelings or indicators for you that trigger your awareness of when you are not Being Here Now? Know that when you experience these feelings, the quality of your thinking is keeping you from Being Here Now.

During these times, you may want to slow down, take a deep breath, acknowledge the distractions and find ways that work for you to clear your mind. Take a walk, look at a picture of a loved one or a favorite vacation spot, or close your eyes and count backwards from 10 (or from 100 if you're really stressed out). Do anything that works for you to interrupt the pattern of your thoughts.

Most importantly, relish those times when you are in the moment, and accept the fact that you are human.

be here now reminders

Another way to improve Being Here Now is through reminders. Many people place "Be Here Now" signs in visible spots to remind them to focus on the person or activity they are involved with at the time. One man placed a sign in his garage so that every time he returned home, he would be reminded to leave work at work.

CALVIN AND HOBBES; ©1994 Watterson Reprinted with permission of Universal Press Syndicate. All rights reserved.

J. W. Metcalf, in his educational video entitled Humor, Risk, Change™ [6], talks about a technique he calls "draw the line," a ceremony or ritual that reminds you to leave work behind when you go home. One example in the video is a man who makes a list of all the work-related issues he might think about when he gets home. He then puts the list in a drawer in his desk, closes the drawer and locks it. As he backs out of his office, he points at the drawer and shouts, "Stay!" Another example is a woman who listens to different comedy recordings in her car on the way home, reminding herself to forget about work and shift gears to home life.

senn delaney
the culture-shaping firm

HEIDRICK & STRUGGLES   © 1994-2017 Senn Delaney Leadership Consulting Group, LLC. All rights reserved.

summary

In summary, to spend more time in the moment:

- Know what the experience of Be Here Now feels like and what it does for you and others.

- Have faith that the more time you spend experiencing the value of Be Here Now, the more you will want to "be there"; consequently, you will begin to "be there" more often.

- Understand the connection between Be Here Now and distractions: Be aware of what gets in the way of Be Here Now.

- Be cautious when your moods/feelings tell you that you're not Being Here Now.

- Understand and accept that everyone goes in and out of the state of Be Here Now.

senn delaney
the culture-shaping firm

HEIDRICK & STRUGGLES

© 1994-2017 Senn Delaney Leadership Consulting Group, LLC. All rights reserved.

questions, action steps and assignments

1. What are some typical distractions that might prevent you from being able to listen to others at a deep level?

_____

_____

_____

_____

_____

2. Identify the key feelings you experience when you are Being Here Now, and those feelings you experience when you are not. When you become aware of these feelings in the future, they will help you identify your state.

_____

_____

_____

_____

_____

3. Establish some Be Here Now reminders that will help you at home and at work.

_____

_____

_____

_____

_____

senn delaney
the culture-shaping firm

HEIDRICK & STRUGGLES

© 1994-2017 Senn Delaney Leadership Consulting Group, LLC. All rights reserved.

3

at your best

Have you ever noticed that there are times you are at your best, and you feel like you can do no wrong? Things just seem to go your way. Your comments are right on target, your ideas are on the money. When faced with pressing deadlines, you are able to focus and get the job done. When faced with problems, you seem to be able to come up with brilliant solutions. Working with others is easy and effortless.

Have you experienced times when you're just off your game? During times like these, we seem to be a step behind everyone else. Our comments and ideas are off the mark. We just can't get "with it"; can't get momentum to get our jobs done. We are easily irritated and the innocent comments of others seem to carry some malevolent hidden meaning.

We all have good times and bad times, and those in between. It is the ebb and flow of life. There are times when we are at our best and times when we are not.

Some people refer to being at your best as being "in the zone," or feeling like you're "on top your game." In this state, we tend to have more perspective. We aren't as locked into our own opinions or limited by our biases. We are more creative in our thinking and not as driven by our egos. We are better able to listen and more responsive to the moment. What does that state feel like for you? How does it impact your effectiveness and your relationships?

Then there are those times when we're at our worst. Some people describe this state as being "in a funk" or "having the weight of the world on our shoulders." What does it feel like for you? What is your thinking like during those times?

mental eddies

When we are at our worst, it can feel like we are literally caught in a vortex of low-quality thoughts. Our thinking is repetitious and circular, and it seems as though we have no control over our thoughts, our feelings or even our circumstances.

© 1994-2017 Senn Delaney Leadership Consulting Group, LLC. All rights reserved.

HEIDRICK & STRUGGLES

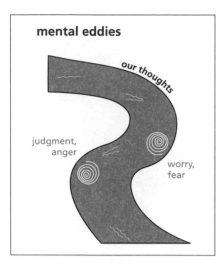

This "mental eddy" sends our spirits into a downward spiral and we lose all perspective. Because we're operating less effectively, our results are diminished, which contributes to our low spirit.

If we could just "let go" and somehow end the cycle of our thinking, then our innate wisdom would naturally and easily rise to the surface.

We all have the same innate capacity to be at our best and have creative insights. This source of brilliance is available to us at any time. When we are caught up in low-quality thinking, access is more difficult; it feels like we're struggling against ourselves. When we are operating in a healthy, high-performance state, access to our innate wisdom is easy and effortless.

When we are at our best, we are:

- Resourceful
- Creative
- Articulate
- Energized
- Focused
- More present
- More patient
- More grateful for life

What is it that makes us so much more effective?

capacities of the mind

When we are at our best, it seems as though we are smarter somehow.

In a way, we are. In his book, *Emotional Intelligence: Why It Can Matter More than IQ*, Daniel Goleman says, "In flow, the brain is in a 'cool' state, its arousal and inhibition of neural circuitry attuned to the demand of the moment…the zone of flow and optimal performance is an oasis of cortical efficiency."[7] In this state, our brains are less distracted by extraneous cortical activity and can operate at peak effectiveness.

© 1994-2017 Senn Delaney Leadership Consulting Group, LLC. All rights reserved.

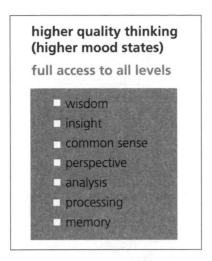

As the diagram above illustrates, higher-quality thinking allows us the capacity to access a whole spectrum of knowledge, including such things as creativity, wisdom and common sense, as well as the ability to use our memory and process information. In the state of being at our best, we are able to access our innate capacity to learn.

During times when we are **not** at our best, we have limited access to our innate wisdom. We are left only with the ability to process the same information from our memory, over and over again.

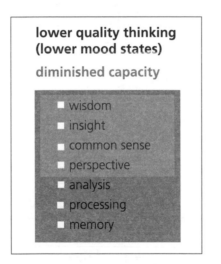

Given that it is human nature for the quality of our thinking to fluctuate, it is not possible to be in a high-quality thinking state all the time. However, there are some things that can help you be aware of the quality of your thinking in any given moment, and that can often help to break the cycle of those spinning, repetitive thoughts.

Below are some "pointers" to living life at your best. As you begin to gain an understanding of these concepts, you will find that your ability to maintain perspective, make better decisions and produce better results will increase naturally, without a lot of stress and effort.

pointer #1: use your feelings as your guide—the mood elevator

We've described in various chapters of this book how your feelings are an indicator of the quality of your thinking. We use the Mood Elevator diagram on the following page to depict this phenomenon. As the quality of our thinking rises, so do our moods and feelings.

© 1994-2017 Senn Delaney Leadership Consulting Group, LLC. All rights reserved.

HEIDRICK & STRUGGLES

Another way to describe this connection is that our feelings work like a barometer: just as a barometer measures atmospheric pressure to indicate the quality of the weather, our moods measure our thinking to indicate the quality of our perspective.

When a barometer rises, it usually indicates that the weather is clear; likewise, when our position on the Mood Elevator rises, it indicates our thinking is clear. We are able to see things with perspective and are less likely to take things personally or blow things out of proportion. Perhaps we are even able to find some humor in the situation, and laugh at ourselves or our circumstances. These thoughts can be trusted, and we can safely act on them with some assurance that our behavior will probably have positive results.

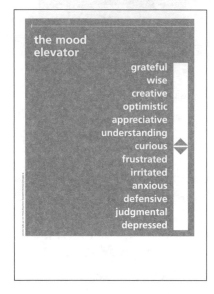

the mood elevator

grateful
wise
creative
optimistic
appreciative
understanding
curious
frustrated
irritated
anxious
defensive
judgmental
depressed

When the barometer drops, it indicates cloudy or stormy weather is ahead. When our moods drop, it indicates that our thinking is clouded as well. We lose sight of the big picture, and everything seems darker and more intense. We take ourselves and our situations very seriously.

These feelings let you know that you need to take some precautions before venturing out. When going out in rainy weather, we make adjustments: We dress more warmly; we drive more slowly; we try to be more focused and careful. Likewise, if you become aware that you are caught up in low-quality thinking, you should be cautious about acting on your thoughts. Delay decision-making if possible, or get input from others.

What are the feelings that signal high-quality thinking for you? Which ones signal low-quality thinking?

unhealthy normal

Sometimes a mood or feeling is so common that it's almost invisible to us.

It's like living close to a freeway. While the traffic noise may bother you at first, after a while you become accustomed to it. The noise is still there, but you don't notice it as much. A recent study by a Cornell University environment psychologist and his European co-authors reports, however, that chronic exposure to low-level traffic noise increases stress levels and blood pressure.[8]

It can be the same with moods. People may comment about our "bad mood," and we are perplexed. We think, "What do they mean? I'm in a perfectly normal mood." In reality, our low

senn delaney
the culture-shaping firm

HEIDRICK & STRUGGLES   © 1994-2017 Senn Delaney Leadership Consulting Group, LLC. All rights reserved.

mood state has become a habit. We call this state "unhealthy normal." Learning to recognize your unhealthy normal thinking habits can help you be at your best more often.

Perhaps your unhealthy normal is impatience; you may have told yourself that you just move a little faster than most people do. Perhaps it's worry, because you feel that you have so much to deal with right now. Whatever the justification, when we rationalize our low mood states, we give credence to the low-quality thinking that causes them and they become self-perpetuating. These low-quality thoughts become chronic "noise" in our brains, causing us added stress and tension.

Fortunately, moving away from unhealthy normal is not nearly as hard as moving to a new house or apartment, away from the freeway—no packing is required. The key is simply a better awareness of your moods and feelings.

Although your unhealthy normal mood may have become difficult for you to recognize, there are usually clues that you're there. How do you feel? While you may not feel like you're in a "bad mood," can you honestly say you're at your best? Are your thoughts persistent and circular? Is your energy level high or low? Do you feel hopeful or defeated?

Think about what unhealthy normal might look like for you.

when it's all about me

Another clue that we're not at our best is the "me" factor. When we feel like "it's all about me," that's when we know we are experiencing lower-quality thinking.

When we're at our best, we tend to have goodwill towards others. We have feelings of gratitude, patience or compassion for the people we encounter. We instinctively understand that they are doing the best they can, just as we are. When we're at our best, we feel like a part of a larger community.

At our worst, we tend to focus more on ourselves.

Our thoughts tend to focus on things like how hard it is for me; what this person or those people did to me; or what's in this for me? We regard others with irritation, frustration or impatience. We often think that other people do not understand what we are going through. We may feel that they are either consciously or unconsciously contributing to our bad mood. Have you ever felt like you

© 1994-2017 Senn Delaney Leadership Consulting Group, LLC. All rights reserved.

had to do everything all by yourself? Or like the whole world was out to get you? When we're at our worst, it's all about "me."

Next time you're "me-deep" in thought, notice what this thinking is doing to your mood, and consider how effective you are given your state of mind.

pointer #2: know your thinking is unreliable in low mood states

Have you ever said or done something in a low mood and afterwards wished you hadn't? Have you sent an e-mail when on a lower floor of the Mood Elevator and later wished you hadn't? We have all done that at one time or another. It happens because our thinking is almost always unreliable when we are in a low mood state. When we are overly impatient, too judgmental, irritated or angry, we lose perspective and common sense. We have low emotional intelligence, or EQ.

Sometimes our low-quality thinking is about us—how tough or unfair things are, or how life doesn't look as good. In addition to the other pointers in the chapter, it can help to simply realize your thinking is unreliable and know that it will look different in time, even after a good night's sleep. It's like watching a scary movie and feeling fear but still knowing it's a movie. And we all live in our own movies, which we create by our thinking each day.

Sometimes our low-quality thinking is about others. We assume motives and judge them harshly, only to see them in a different light when perspective returns.

www.cartoonstock.com

What's the answer to "doing down well"; to doing the least damage to ourselves and others when we are down? The answer is simple but not necessarily easy: Don't trust or act on your thinking in a low mood state.

This is easier to do when you are aware that your thinking is unreliable. The challenge is that our thinking always seems real to us, no matter how off it may be. In fact, when we feel most righteous or most compelled to say or do something, it is often the worst time to say or do anything.

That takes us back to using our feelings as our guide. An analogy one of our consultants created is the "icy road guideline." If you had to go out on a dark night with icy roads, you would know to drive with care and not make sudden moves. When you're in a low mood, remember the icy road, and act and speak more carefully.

senn delaney
the culture-shaping firm

HEIDRICK & STRUGGLES   © 1994-2017 Senn Delaney Leadership Consulting Group, LLC. All rights reserved.

There are times when everyone is thrown by their troubles and loses their bearings. It's human nature. Learning to recognize the quality of our thinking, and understanding how it affects us, is what gives us mental traction. We become better able to keep our bearings in stressful situations.

pointer #3: know that it's your thinking, not "them"

The underlying principle of these concepts is that our thinking creates our experience of life. It is a simple yet profound shift in our basic approach to living. We call this approach "inside-out" versus "outside-in."

Many times in life, it appears to us that outside circumstances, situations and other people's actions "make" us feel and act a certain way.

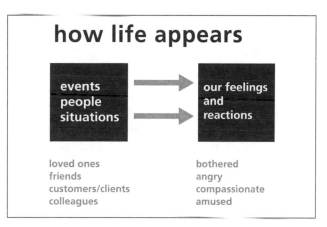

This is really not a very hopeful way of looking at life. In this mode, we place our experience of life more in the hands of other people and circumstances or situations outside of ourselves. It's more of an "outside-in" approach to life.

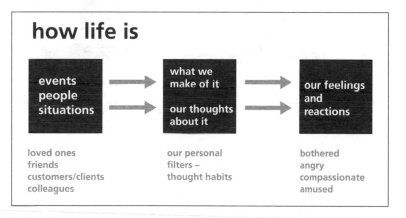

In reality, our feelings are caused by what our thinking makes of the event, not the event itself.

It is our thinking that causes the feeling and it is the feeling that creates the experience. It happens so fast we don't even know it's happened at all. In fact, the human brain perceives all thought as being real, much like the special effects in a movie. For instance, when we watch a scene in a movie where someone is in danger, sometimes we notice our own heart is actually beating faster. Our brain perceives our fear as real, and sends "fear" signals to our bodies, even though the event is not actually happening to us.

© 1994-2017 Senn Delaney Leadership Consulting Group, LLC. All rights reserved.

senn delaney
the culture-shaping firm

HEIDRICK & STRUGGLES

There is ample proof of this phenomenon in our everyday life. Have you ever had a loved one do something one day and it was cute or amusing—and yet the exact same thing irritated you another day?

Or perhaps you've noticed situations where two people were faced with almost the exact same set of stressful circumstances and they reacted very differently. One person practically seemed to lose their sanity over it, while the other took it in stride.

> "I remember being shocked when our whole department was given notice that we were being laid off. I was even more shocked when I heard Lou from our department talking about it. He has young kids just like I do, but he spoke of it as a 'blessing in disguise.' He was looking forward to trying something new. On the other hand, I was mad. Mad at the company and mad at the world for dealing me this blow. I eventually got a new job and wound up okay, but it took me a lot longer than Lou."

Understanding this phenomenon and being willing to accept that it is our own thinking that ultimately creates our experience of life can help us deal with people and events much more effectively. At first this approach can feel like a burden, since it means taking full accountability for our own experience of life. But in the long-term, this approach gives us more control over our lives, our behavior and results. The "inside-out" approach is much more hopeful.

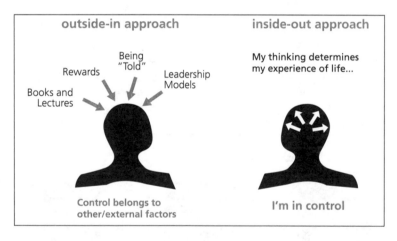

pointer #4: take better care of yourself

During the unfreezing session, we shook hands with everyone in the room at top speed to illustrate the importance of energy for individuals, teams and cultures. In their book, *The Power of Full Engagement: Managing Energy, Not Time, is the Key to High Performance and Personal Renewal*, Jim Loehr and Tony Schwartz, who have worked with thousands of athletes and executives, contend that in today's world managing energy is more important than managing time. "Full engagement requires cultivating a dynamic balance between the expenditure of energy (stress) and the renewal of energy (recovery) in all dimensions."[9] Whether executives or athletes, "we grow at all levels by expending energy beyond our normal limits, and then recovering."[10] For far too many executives, the stress is there but not the recovery.

Have you noticed that when you are fatigued and stressed, you are less patient, more easily bothered and more critical of others? We are less resilient, less creative and less resourceful when we are not at our best physically.

HEIDRICK & STRUGGLES   © 1994-2017 Senn Delaney Leadership Consulting Group, LLC. All rights reserved.

Fatigue and lack of energy affects our brain functions, thereby affecting the quality of our thinking and our moods. Making sure you maintain a healthy diet and get plenty of sleep and adequate exercise will help keep your body and your brain functioning well. In fact, endorphins released during exercise have a profound impact on your overall sense of well being. Exercise also causes you to focus on something different, which temporarily quiets the mind of any low-quality thoughts.

So don't think you are benefiting yourself or your organization by burning yourself out. You can accomplish far more in less time when you are at your best physically and mentally. Develop a plan that allows you to stretch and recover. Invest time in yourself so you can be the best you can be.

www.comics.com

pointer #5: try pattern interrupts

Since the quality of your thinking determines your effectiveness and the quality of your life, it pays to find ways to shift your thinking or quiet your mind when you are low on the Mood Elevator.

Step one is to become more aware of when you are irritated, worried, judgmental, angry, bothered or depressed. Since your thinking causes that, Step two is to break out of that thought pattern. The sooner you recognize the feeling flare up, the easier it is to deflect it. It may be as simple as saying to yourself, "Don't go there," taking a deep, relaxing breath versus acting out.

Each person needs to find their own "pattern interrupt" that can take them out of lower-quality thinking. Try exercising, taking a walk, engaging in something you really like or that you've found takes your mind out of its thought patterns. Effective pattern interrupts can help us in all aspects of life, not just work. They can include hobbies (such as gardening), sports and being with positive people. Even a small break can quiet the mind enough to gain a fresh outlook.

pointer #6: assume positive intentions

Imagine for a moment that you're driving down the highway on a relaxing sunny day. Suddenly a sports car zooms past on your right, cuts in front of you just a little too closely and then speeds off.

What might you think in this situation? How might you react? You may assume the driver was behaving with selfish disregard for others and hope that he is caught and cited for reckless driving. You'd probably feel your anger or irritation was justified.

Now imagine that several minutes later, as you take the next exit and approach the stoplight, you see the same car next to you. You look over, either out of curiosity or to make eye contact and let them know that they put you out. You see a young man behind the wheel, sweating profusely—and just beyond him you see his pregnant wife holding her large tummy, trying to breathe away the

© 1994-2017 Senn Delaney Leadership Consulting Group, LLC. All rights reserved.

pain—and realize that both of them are only focused on getting her to the hospital on time.

How would your thoughts and feelings change about the situation? Now, you might have compassion for the people in the car, or some embarrassment that you misjudged them. Now, you'd probably hope that they make it on time, and wish them the best.

What was the difference between the two states of mind in the above example? The first attitude was affected by an assumption about the man's intentions. When you realized that his intentions were not what you thought, you were able to feel compassion toward him.

How often do we make assumptions about other people's intentions? As human beings, we assume things on a daily basis; in fact, we need to make certain assumptions just to get through the day. Sometimes our assumptions are accurate and effective—and sometimes they aren't. The very nature of assumptions is that at the time we make them, they do not feel like assumptions at all; they simply feel right. However, have you ever assumed something only to find out later that you were wrong? Have you ever taken action on an incorrect assumption with an unintended and very negative consequence?

The chart shown below illustrates how our assumptions affect our reactions and the likely results on our relationships with others, based on how they will see us. You will notice that the reactions from assumption of innocence/positive intent mirror the states of mind at the higher end of the mood elevator. In more cases than not, those assumptions are more accurate. People are rarely trying deliberately to irritate us; they are just being who they are.

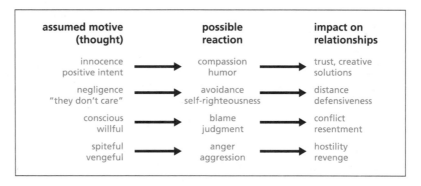

Assuming innocence or positive intent doesn't mean that the person is necessarily innocent of the actions they took, or that you should ignore the behavior. It means understanding that **people are just doing what makes sense to them based on their own thinking**. In that frame of mind, we can approach situations with perspective, which helps us determine the truth and decide on the best course of action.

pointer #7: gratitude perspective

The most powerful perspective we can have is a gratitude perspective. When we are in the lower mood states, it always means we have lost our perspective. Our problems become our whole world because they consume our thinking. Later, we almost always wonder why it seemed like such a big deal. The gratitude model helps explain this.

HEIDRICK & STRUGGLES   © 1994-2017 Senn Delaney Leadership Consulting Group, LLC. All rights reserved.

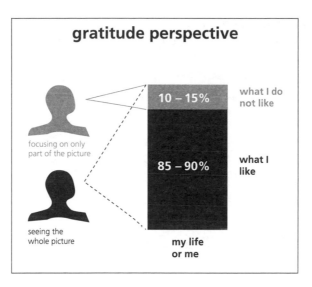

The bar in the above graphic represents "My Life or Me." Most of us appreciate 80-90% of our lives. And most of us feel there is 10-15% of our life that we would like to be different.

Many people spend a lot of time and energy focusing on the 10-15% they don't like. As you can imagine, that experience is stressful, frustrating and unfulfilling. It is much more effective, not to mention more accurate, to look at the total picture. This does not mean we should ignore the 10-20% that we don't like, but that we should see it as only a small percentage of the whole. It is much easier to maintain perspective when we appreciate the 85-90%, and that perspective makes us more effective as we work on improving or accepting the parts we don't like.

Deborah Norville, the news journalist and author, wrote an interesting bestselling book called *Thank You Power: Making the Science of Gratitude Work for You*. She cited research from a University of California study that showed the benefits received by people who cultivated a daily attitude of gratitude, as opposed to groups who focused on problems. "The people who focused on gratitude were just flat-out happier. They saw their lives in favorable terms. They reported fewer negative physical symptoms, such as headaches or colds, and they were active in ways that were good for them."[11]

"Counting your blessings" is more than a platitude; it's a good, common-sense way to maintain your perspective.

summary

None of us is at our best all the time. To the extent that we can take an "inside-out" approach to life, as opposed to "outside-in," we will gain a greater appreciation of the times we are at our best, and a greater ability to maintain perspective when we're not.

Here is a summary of pointers to spend more time at your best:

- **Use your feelings, or moods, as a guide to the quality of your thinking.** Higher mood states indicate clear, high-quality thinking. Low moods indicate low-quality thinking. Learn to identify your unhealthy normal, or a lower mood state that has become habit.

- **Don't trust or act on your thoughts when you're in a low mood state.** Acting on low-quality thoughts leads to a downward spiral of low-quality behavior and results. Be cautious and remember that "this, too, shall pass."

© 1994-2017 Senn Delaney Leadership Consulting Group, LLC. All rights reserved.

- **Know that your thinking creates your reality.** Everything we experience is processed by our brain first, and delivered to us via thought. Since the quality of our thinking varies, so will our experience of life.

- **Take better care of yourself.** Our mental state is tied to our physical state. Rest, exercise and a healthy diet help us to be more resilient and less prone to low mood states.

- **Try pattern interrupts.** Change your thinking—change your mood.

- **Maintain perspective.** Remember that gratitude is the express button to the top of the Mood Elevator and that laughter lifts your spirits.

questions, action steps and assignments

1. What does it feel like for you when you are at your best? What is the nature of your thinking?

_____

_____

_____

2. What are your feelings and thinking like when you're at your worst?

_____

_____

_____

3. What does unhealthy normal look like for you? What are some clues that you're there?

_____

_____

_____

4. Think about your overall mental health. Are there ways you can adjust your lifestyle slightly to improve your outlook?

_____

_____

_____

5. List some pattern interrupts that might work for you when you feel your thoughts becoming circular.

_____

_____

_____

6. Make a list of the things in your life for which you are especially grateful.

_____

_____

_____

_____

senn delaney
the culture-shaping firm

HEIDRICK & STRUGGLES   © 1994-2017 Senn Delaney Leadership Consulting Group, LLC. All rights reserved.

4

behavioral styles

better understanding the filters through which we see the world

We often assume that others see the world the way we do, and under normal circumstances, act and think as we would. When people do not behave in a way that seems normal to us, we think something's wrong with them; they're being selfish, contrary or overly emotional. Studies in behavioral styles show us that these assumptions are not only false, but they can limit our ability to deal with others effectively.

There are fundamental differences in how people see the world around them and how they react to it. Some combination of inborn tendencies and life experiences creates our thought habits, which determine our behavioral habits, personality or thinking style. Naturally, it is not possible to know the tendencies and habits of every person we deal with on a daily basis.

But as we begin to understand the differences in the styles of people with whom we interact, we become more effective in dealing with challenges and better able to accept and coach them with less judgment. In fact, judgment is a primary barrier to productive relationships, and removing that barrier can allow communication to flow more freely. As we begin to accept people for who they are and what they believe, it creates an environment of trust, respect and openness.

characteristics of behavioral styles

Earlier in this book and in the unfreezing session, we discussed the **Human Operating System** and the concept of **filters**: how our experiences, values, beliefs, thought habits and interests shape our worldview and create our own unique set of filters. This set of filters, which gives us each our own unique thinking style, also forms our own unique **behavioral style**.

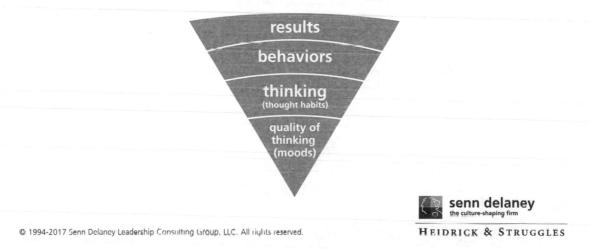

© 1994-2017 Senn Delaney Leadership Consulting Group, LLC. All rights reserved.

senn delaney
the culture-shaping firm

HEIDRICK & STRUGGLES

The results cone shows how these various filters drive our behaviors and, ultimately, our results.

The behavioral style framework gives us a tool to understand the reality that we all see the world differently, and therefore, we all have a different approach to getting results.

We've found that most people fall within four major behavioral styles. While most people display elements of different styles at different times, people generally are inclined to have a single default or "home-base" style. Because each style tends to have different thought habits, which result in different behavioral habits, people can usually be identified by the behavioral elements of their style.

Read the following descriptions and see which fits you best, and which may describe some of your teammates.

Controlling Style

Theme: Tends to take charge, is decisive and bottom-line focused

Strengths/Pluses:

- Strong-willed
- Self-motivated
- Results-focused
- Initiates activities
- Task-oriented; businesslike demeanor

Approach to Work:

- Bottom-line focused
- Direct in dealing with people
- Decisive
- Concerned with efficiency
- Task accomplisher

Challenges/Minuses:

- Impatient
- Can be too dominant
- Not sensitive to feelings
- Demanding
- Unwilling to "let go"

Supporting Style

Theme: Tends to be relationship-oriented, is a team player and consensus builder

Strengths/Pluses:

- Loyal and people-oriented
- Understanding and empathetic

HEIDRICK & STRUGGLES　　　　　　© 1994-2017 Senn Delaney Leadership Consulting Group, LLC. All rights reserved.

- Cooperative and flexible
- Willing to be of service
- Patient—good listener

Approach to Work:

- Good team builder
- Good at reconciling factions that might be in conflict
- Builds relationships to get the job done
- Dedicated and committed
- Cause-oriented

Challenges/Minuses:

- Confronting people
- Saying "no"
- Creating processes
- Focusing on results
- Dealing with critical and aggressive people

Promoting Style

Theme: Tends to be stimulating and inspirational; radiates excitement for new ideas

Strengths/Pluses:

- Energetic
- Adventurous
- Creative
- Persuasive
- Enjoys new and different challenges
- Spontaneous

Approach to Work:

- Good at motivating and inspiring others
- Expresses ideas and opinions persuasively
- Quick to action
- "Big picture" thinker
- Imaginative

Challenges/Minuses:

- May avoid details and data
- Lack of planning and follow-through

© 1994-2017 Senn Delaney Leadership Consulting Group, LLC All rights reserved.

- Does too much at once
- Could use more structure
- Can be too impulsive

Analyzing Style

Theme: Tends to be thorough, organized and a good planner

Strengths/Pluses:

- Planning and organization
- Conscientious and logical
- Persistent and steady
- Following through
- Setting up systems and procedures

Approach to work:

- Problem solver
- Thorough/accurate
- Reliable and dependable
- Anchor of reality
- Defines and clarifies problems and issues

Challenges/Minuses:

- Can be indecisive
- Too detailed
- Risk-averse; overly cautious
- Not expressive/persuasive enough
- Overly process-oriented

value of the behavioral style framework

Understanding the tendencies and preferences of the four styles framework also helps us:

- Build on our own strengths and work on our challenges.
- Understand the strengths and challenges of others so that we can better lead and manage them.
- Understand that actions which seem strange to us may simply reflect the characteristics of the thinking and behavioral style of the other person.
- Avoid judgment by seeing the innocence in people's actions, accepting that they are doing the best they can given their thinking; that they are just exhibiting the characteristics of their style.

senn delaney
the culture-shaping firm

HEIDRICK & STRUGGLES

© 1994-2017 Senn Delaney Leadership Consulting Group, LLC. All rights reserved.

- Gain more respect for the differences of others. Understanding styles can be the first step to understanding other differences such as gender, ethnic origin, age, religion or sexual orientation.

understanding strengths and style tendencies

Each of us has a home-base style with many positive characteristics, and each style also has a number of potential challenges. Every style can also encounter problems if it is overused or overextended. Here is a quick look at the potential strengths and challenges of each style:

	Strengths	If Overused
Controlling	Take charge, determined, decisive, results-oriented, efficient	Autocratic, insensitive, impatient, over-controlling, poor listening skills
Supporting	Team players, friendly, good listeners, relationship-oriented, conscientious	Too tolerant, unassertive, non-confronting, too driven to please
Promoting	Stimulating, goal-driven, enthusiastic, innovative, risk takers	Poor at planning, ego-driven, undisciplined, poor at follow-up
Analyzing	Thorough, detailed, rational, organized, good planners	Indecisive, too detailed, aloof, risk-averse, not intuitive

Which cartoon goes with which style?

"Yes I do, and so does he."

www.cartoonstock.com

Controlling

"For heaven's sake, all I asked is which do you want, a hamburger or a lamb chop?"

© The New Yorker Collection 1988 Barney Tobey from cartoonbank.com All Rights Reserved.

Controlling
Analyzing

senn delaney
the culture-shaping firm

© 1994-2017 Senn Delaney Leadership Consulting Group, LLC. All rights reserved.

HEIDRICK & STRUGGLES

"Never mind the song and dance, Higgins.
What about the Atkins account?"

© The New Yorker Collection 1985 Frank Modell from cartoonbank.com. All Rights Reserved.

"Somebody needs a hug."

www.cartoonstock.com

blending multiple styles

Did you see traits of yours in more than one style? Many people do. While we may spend more time in our home-base style, which is our most comfortable position, we all flex a bit. In addition, many people have a home base "close to the line." This means that they have tendencies of two adjacent quadrants. You might be a controlling style with many promoting tendencies, or an analyzer with a number of supporting tendencies. Rarely, however, do people have strong tendencies in the opposite, or diagonal, quadrant.

complement or conflict?

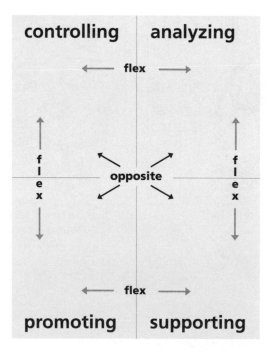

The largest potential for conflict or judgment is in the opposite diagonal quadrants. That is because these styles see the world and what is important so differently. We like to view this as complemen-

senn delaney
the culture-shaping firm

HEIDRICK & STRUGGLES

© 1994-2017 Senn Delaney Leadership Consulting Group, LLC. All rights reserved.

tary quadrants since the strengths of each are perfect complements for the weaknesses of the other. Therefore, there are important lessons they can learn from each other.

Controlling-Style Lessons

Controlling-style people have the greatest challenges with those from the supporting-style quadrant. They can be more effective in working with and leading the supporting style by showing that they care, and by providing specific plans with details about activities to be accomplished. They could also be more effective by being less concerned about being right all the time.

Controlling-style people operate best when they are measured by results and goals attained and being allowed to take charge where possible. When working with others, controlling-style people should discuss performance measures and clarify roles and responsibilities.

Supporting-Style Lessons

Supporting-style people have the greatest challenges with those from the controlling-style quadrant. They can be more effective in working with and leading the controlling style by allowing them freedom to do things their own way, and recognizing that they don't like having their time wasted or decisions being made without their input.

Supporting-style people can help others work more effectively with them by letting others know that they value positive cooperation and do better when given structure with goals and methods for achieving each goal.

Promoting-Style Lessons

Promoting-style people have the greatest challenges with those from the analyzing-style quadrant. They can be more effective in working with and leading the analyzing style by providing more data and information and being better prepared. Promoting-style people should recognize that the analyzing style doesn't like being pressured or cornered into making decisions without time for gathering data. Promoting-style people could also be more effective in leading or working with the analyzing style by establishing a framework or track for them to follow.

Promoting-style people can help others work more effectively with them by letting others know that they need fresh challenges, value recognition and feedback, and appreciate when others share their enthusiasm for projects on the table. Promoting-style people can improve their personal effectiveness by shoring up their ability to create a framework and structure toward reaching their goals.

Analyzing-Style Lessons

Analyzing-style people have the greatest challenges with those from the promoting-style quadrant. They can be more effective in working with and leading the promoting style by getting excited with them and showing emotion. Analyzing-style people should recognize that the promoting style feels rewarded by applause, feedback and recognition, and they like to be challenged. Analyzing-style people can lead promoters more effectively by inspiring them to bigger and better accomplishments.

Analyzing-style people can help others work more effectively with them by letting others know that they like to get as much information and data as possible and to make decisions at their own pace without feeling cornered or pressured. A high-impact growth area for the analyzing style is to work on interpersonal and communication skills.

© 1994-2017 Senn Delaney Leadership Consulting Group, LLC. All rights reserved.

managing conflict

Conflict often arises when we are unable to understand and appreciate another person's style or the way that they approach life. Sometimes the differences in style are so great that we feel like the dog in the cartoon below:

"May I offer a very different scenario?"

© The New Yorker Collection 1989 Peter Steiner from cartoonbank.com. All Rights Reserved.

The following list points out some major areas of conflict and describes ways to reduce or avoid conflict:

Controlling-style people are frustrated by the lack of urgency in others and irritated by overly emotional or sensitive people.

Resolution: They would gain most by tuning in to their own feelings and the feelings of those around them. They would gain much by letting go of the need to be right.

Supporting-style people are uncomfortable around aggressive people and go to great lengths to avoid conflict.

Resolution: They would gain most if they would be more results-oriented with themselves and others, and see conflict as a way of working through differences rather than a personal attack.

Promoting-style people dislike indecisiveness and dealing with large amounts of boring data.

Resolution: They would gain most by realizing the payoff that comes with slowing down, looking at available data and following through on commitments.

Analyzing-style people are turned off by hype, exaggerations and excitement without facts.

Resolution: They would gain most by understanding how to limit analysis, take a few risks and be more enthusiastic.

tips for dealing with different styles

When you are able to recognize another's style and adapt to it in a way that improves communication between you, it is called style flexing. You are basically **speaking the language** the other person understands.

senn delaney
the culture-shaping firm

HEIDRICK & STRUGGLES   © 1994-2017 Senn Delaney Leadership Consulting Group, LLC. All rights reserved.

Here are some guidelines on how to adapt to each style:

Controlling

To deal most effectively with the controlling style, realize that they tend to focus on **results**. Try to communicate in an efficient, results-oriented manner. Be willing to state your opinions clearly but allow the controlling person to have the final say. Briefly:

- Get to the point, be specific.
- Keep the conversation focused on end results.
- Do not waste time; speak and act quickly.
- Provide options for them to choose.
- Provide overview, but have details available if needed.
- Be decisive and self-confident.
- Let them make the final decision.

Supporting

To deal most effectively with the supporting style, realize that they tend to focus on **relationships**. Try to respect their feelings and be supportive of their relationships with others. Do your best to make them feel that they are part of the team. Avoid force and authority; understanding and respect are more effective. Briefly:

- Show sincere interest in them and their feelings.
- Be cooperative rather than pushy.
- Be patient; draw out their ideas and concerns.
- Gently explore areas of disagreement; avoid open conflict.
- Be encouraging; build their confidence.
- Spend time on the relationship before jumping into the task.

Promoting

To deal most effectively with the promoting style, realize that they thrive on **excitement**. They love new ideas, people and projects. Try to support their ideas and aspirations and give them recognition. They like to look good in the eyes of others. It helps to appeal to their need for enthusiasm, ideas and goals. Briefly:

- Allow time for exploring mutually exciting possibilities.
- Let them do most of the talking.
- Avoid arguing; if you disagree, look for alternative solutions.
- Look at the big picture and avoid bogging down in details.
- Make your presentation stimulating and exciting.
- Be open to their new ideas.

Analyzing

To deal most effectively with the analyzing style, realize that their primary focus tends to be on **data and facts**. This tendency is driven by their need to make accurate decisions. Try to show them that

© 1994-2017 Senn Delaney Leadership Consulting Group, LLC. All rights reserved

senn delaney
the culture-shaping firm

HEIDRICK & STRUGGLES

you value accurate information and will not jump to conclusions. It's helpful to present facts and data rather than ideas and opinions, and give them enough time to work through all the details before they are asked for a decision. Briefly:

- Avoid surprises.
- Be patient: cover each item thoroughly.
- Be organized and logical; avoid hype.
- Give them time to get comfortable with the situation.
- Ask their help in finding the facts.
- Minimize risks.

One woman participant shared how her insights regarding behavioral styles improved her effectiveness in working with others:

> "I've recognized for a long time that I have a controlling style. I've been reminded several times of my somewhat abrasive, no-nonsense manner of 'getting the job done.' I'd get impatient and judgmental with people because I assumed my style was the right one.

> "Now I realize that it is good that there are different styles. I have a better understanding of people with different styles and don't get as impatient. I learned how to better communicate with people of a different style, which has led to more effective relations and better results. I discovered it really doesn't 'hurt' either. In fact, it feels pretty good."

the balanced organization

In a balanced organization, a diverse group of people works together and benefits from their different perceptions, experiences, educational focus and styles. Their individual differences contribute to a better whole. The following chart shows some primary contributions of each style:

Controlling	Analyzing
Task accomplisher	Objective, reality-based
Bottom-line results	Conscientious, steady
Self-motivated	Defines and clarifies
Risk taker	Gathers needed data and information
Fast decision maker	Criticizes and tests data
Initiates activities	Maintains standards
Disciplined	Concerned with accuracy

senn delaney
the culture-shaping firm

HEIDRICK & STRUGGLES

© 1994-2017 Senn Delaney Leadership Consulting Group, LLC. All rights reserved.

Promoting	Supporting
High energy, moves quickly	Dedicated and committed
Enjoyable to be around	Loyal team member
Creative imagination	Good listener
Initiates relationships	Patient and sympathetic
Motivating	Keeps peace
Competitive spirit	Cause-oriented
Goal-oriented	Team player

behavioral styles and quality of thinking (moods)

The quality of our thinking and our ability to Be Here Now greatly affects our ability to deal with different behavior styles, because we are more aware of our own thought habits and behavior styles, and can make appropriate adjustments. Being aware of our moods is a key way to gauge the quality of our thinking in the moment.

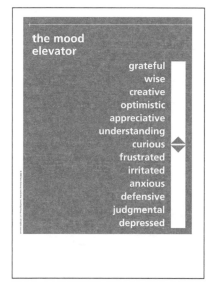

When the quality of our thinking is at a high level, indicated by feelings on the upper end of the Mood Elevator, such as humor, contentment, compassion or gratitude, the differences between behavioral styles seem less obvious and the commonalities become more apparent. It is easier to see the other person's point of view, and why they may react the way they do, as well as to recognize our own "default setting" or the thought habits that lead us to see things the way we do.

Because of this, in the higher mood states we do a better job of shifting toward the appropriate style to match the situation. For example, our understanding may allow us to become more supportive when someone is overwhelmed or more task-focused when a job needs to get done.

Of course, the opposite is also true. In the lower states of the mood elevator, we tend to become caught up in our own thought habits, unable to see or understand the other person is simply exhib-

senn delaney
the culture-shaping firm

© 1994-2017 Senn Delaney Leadership Consulting Group, LLC. All rights reserved.   HEIDRICK & STRUGGLES

iting the characteristics of their own style. We also tend to exhibit the most negative tendencies of our own style.

As we learn to use our moods to identify the quality of our thinking in the moment, we can use the behavioral style framework to enhance our relationships by better managing conflicts with people of other styles and learning how to flex our own style.

summary

Utilizing the behavioral style framework helps you to be more effective. There are three key points that you should keep in mind:

- Know your own primary style as well as its strengths and challenges.

- Increase your ability to adapt to the style of others and speak their style-language.

- Learn to respect the differences in others and the contribution those differences make to the overall effectiveness of the team.

© 1994-2017 Senn Delaney Leadership Consulting Group, LLC. All rights reserved.

questions, action steps and assignments

1. How can you be more effective by using the behavioral style framework?

_____

_____

_____

_____

_____

2. Which style do you have the most difficulty dealing with? How could you be more effective dealing with that style?

_____

_____

_____

_____

3. Have a conversation with your team or group about your individual styles. Have the group give feedback to each other and to you on how they see each other. Have people share how they like to be directed, coached, reviewed and supported. If you do not have direct reports, do this exercise with your boss.

_____

_____

_____

_____

4. Have a conversation with your loved ones about your individual styles. Allow for feedback on how they see you, and vice versa. Have them share with you how they would like to be supported, based on their respective styles. Share with them how you would like to be supported.

_____

_____

_____

_____

© 1994-2017 Senn Delaney Leadership Consulting Group, LLC. All rights reserved.

senn delaney
the culture-shaping firm

HEIDRICK & STRUGGLES

self-scoring behavioral style assessment tool

The following is a short self-scoring behavioral style evaluator to determine your own style or the styles of others. Circle the number and letter that best represents your perception on each scale. Then total the number of each letter and number circled and find the appropriate quadrant in the style matrix.

Go along .... Take charge	Aloof .... Welcoming
D **C** **B** **A**	**1** **2** **3** **4**

Quiet .... Talkative	Calm .... Excitable
D **C** **B** **A**	**1** **2** **3** **4**

Supportive .... Challenging	Reserved ....Animated
D **C** **B** **A**	**1** **2** **3** **4**

Compliant.............................Dominant	Task-oriented...........People-oriented
D **C** **B** **A**	**1** **2** **3** **4**

Asks questions..........Makes statements	Serious ....Friendly, attentive
D **C** **B** **A**	**1** **2** **3** **4**

Cooperative .... Competitive	Talks only business................Shares personal feelings
D **C** **B** **A**	**1** **2** **3** **4**

Introverted.......................... Extroverted	Reserved .... Outgoing
D **C** **B** **A**	**1** **2** **3** **4**

Slow, studied....................... Fast-paced	Wants facts ....Wants opinions
D **C** **B** **A**	**1** **2** **3** **4**

Non-assertive.......................... Assertive	Non-emotional .... Emotional
D **C** **B** **A**	**1** **2** **3** **4**

Constrained............................... Open	Non-responsive.............. Responsive
D **C** **B** **A**	**1** **2** **3** **4**

Total: ☐ ☐ ☐ ☐	Total: ☐ ☐ ☐ ☐
D C B A	1 2 3 4

Find the highest scored letter (A, B, C or D) and the highest scored number (1, 2 3 or 4), then find the corresponding area in the matrix chart by plotting the two points.

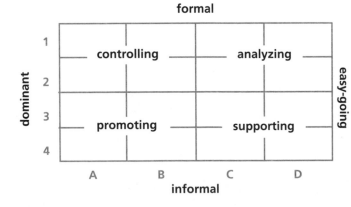

HEIDRICK & STRUGGLES   © 1994-2017 Senn Delaney Leadership Consulting Group, LLC. All rights reserved.

5

the essential value set

the essential values in high-performance teams and cultures

As a result of more than 30 years of work in helping leaders shape their organizational cultures with values and guiding behaviors, we've discovered that there is a set of essential value categories that exist in all successful organizations. We've concluded that these universal principles of life effectiveness are also present in successful individuals and high-performance teams. They can be described in different ways and defined by different words, but the broad categories of the Essential Value Set include the following core values:

- A **performance** value, which has a results focus, high expectations and an emphasis on personal accountability

- A **collaborative** value, which promotes cross-organizational teamwork, mutual support and decisions for the greater good

- A **change** value, which encourages innovation, openness to change, individual and organizational coaching, and mentoring and learning

- An **ethics/integrity** value, which provides an essential foundation for all else

- An **organizational** health value, which creates an energized, open, trusting, respectful, positive, hopeful and optimistic environment

- A **customer** value, which focuses people on the organization's purpose and whom they serve; in contrast to the other values, this element can be covered in the organization's vision/mission as well as in its value set

If an individual, a team or an organization falls short in any one of these categories, results and fulfillment will suffer.

For example, an organization could have a focus on results and high performance expectations, but still fail because they fell short in teamwork and collaboration. In today's complex and interconnected world, implementing any major organization-wide strategy without teamwork or collaboration is difficult, if not impossible. Another organization might assume that they have great values and a great culture because they have high ethics and work together well. While they do have several key elements of a successful culture, if they fall short in accountability and change, they probably won't be results-focused and adaptable enough to ensure long-term success.

In the past, there have been dramatic examples of organizations that excelled in several categories, and yet failed because they were deficient in others. The now-infamous Enron Corporation is a prime example. At its peak, Enron probably outperformed almost every other organization in the

© 1994-2017 Senn Delaney Leadership Consulting Group, LLC. All rights reserved.

HEIDRICK & STRUGGLES

world in the performance and change/innovation values. Their ultimate demise was directly linked to their shortfall in the ethics/integrity value. This happened to a number of high performers that experienced short-term success in the past decade.

On the other hand, we've seen sustained performance over a number of years from companies like Southwest Airlines and Wal-Mart. Time will tell if they can be agile and change-oriented enough to sustain their high performance over the coming years.

You learned about the essential values in many of the exercises you experienced during your unfreezing session.

the performance value:

accountability and empowerment the "make it happen" ingredient

> "For the last two decades, the most exercised part of the corporate body has been the pointed finger!"[12]
>
> Tom Peters

"If it is to be, it is up to me" is the unstated motto of people who live the accountability value. Accountability is the "make it happen" value. It is the point of view that comes from a belief that our individual actions (or inactions), not outside forces, are the major determinant of our success (or lack thereof). When people believe they have a great deal of control over their own destiny, they are proactive in making decisions and influencing outcomes and usually do not become victims of circumstance. Rather than wasting energy complaining, blaming or wishing things were different, they devote their energy to moving forward in spite of obstacles.

When this attitude is prevalent within an organization, results are better because people are not stuck in the past, placing blame or defending why something did not work. They are constantly moving forward, asking themselves, "What more can I do to get the result?"

A culture of accountability is the foundation of any results-producing organization. Lack of accountability, otherwise known as victim behavior, is the greatest energy drain a company can have. In older, more conservative cultures, it often takes the form of entitlement or "the company owes me." In companies facing challenges and struggling for results, it may show up as blaming and excuses as people try to prove "it's not my fault." It also can result in too much time spent complaining about things beyond people's control, or gravity issues.

One person who was particularly moved by this aspect of the unfreezing session created an "accountability version" of the Serenity Prayer (generally attributed to American theologian Reinhold Niebuhr):

> "Grant me the serenity to accept the **people** I cannot change, the courage to change the **person** I can, and the wisdom to know it's **me**."

Empowerment is a related and often misunderstood concept. No matter how much leaders and managers delegate, encourage and work to motivate employees, the ultimate decision to take action, or not, is not the managers', but the employees'. Others cannot empower us. They can help us realize the power we already have, but empowerment is an "inside-out" operation.

In a culture, it is far more powerful to focus on accountability than on empowerment. When accountability is present in an organization, or in an individual or team, it will manifest as: a can-do attitude, a bias for action, persisting through obstacles and second efforts. Accountability is, in fact, self-empowerment.

HEIDRICK & STRUGGLES   © 1994-2017 Senn Delaney Leadership Consulting Group, LLC. All rights reserved.

"I'd like to hear less talk about animal rights
and more talk about animal responsibilities."

© The New Yorker Collection 1990 Lee Lorenz from cartoonbank.com. All Rights Reserved.

the shadow of accountability

To create a more accountable organization, it is important for leaders at all levels to role-model accountability, rather than waste time blaming and complaining. People who do this find it much easier to hold those around them more accountable. When faced with excuses or unproductive conversations about gravity issues, they listen, briefly acknowledge the challenge, and then always ask the accountability question, "What more can we do?" When that behavior becomes a part of the culture, focus shifts from reasons to results.

It often seems like we live in a "victim society." This mindset has become so prevalent in our politics and court systems that it can become invisible to us. One useful tool in recognizing when people are using victim language is the Accountability Ladder. Like the Mood Elevator, the Accountability Ladder has a number of different levels, all characterized by the words people might use based on their current level of accountability.

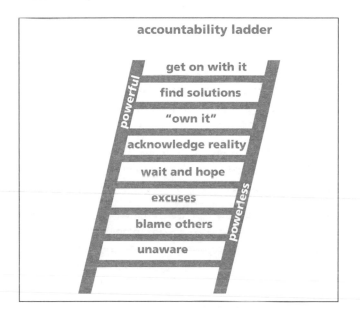

The Accountability Ladder can help you determine your personal level of accountability, and recognize where others might be as well.

senn delaney
the culture-shaping firm

the collaborative value

teamwork: the "optimization" factor

> "The way a team plays as a whole determines its success. You may have the greatest bunch of individual stars in the world, but if they don't play together, the club won't be worth a dime."[13]

Babe Ruth

People can be personally accountable and still be ineffective in the grander scheme of things because they aren't collaborative. In today's complex world, no one can do it all alone. Teamwork is what we call the optimization factor of a high-performance culture. Successful business solutions require interdependence on the part of individuals, functions and business units. Shared services, customer solutions, and implementation of major systems all require cross-organizational collaboration and a willingness to make decisions for the greater good.

Drawing by P. Kleba; ©1994 SDLCG

The collaborative value is often missing because we live in a society that values independence over interdependence. Winning all too often means, "I win," not "we win," as we found in the arm wrestle exercise during the unfreezing session. We tend to have the thought habit, "for me to win, someone else has to lose." That habit leads to silos, turf issues and we-they behaviors.

Without good teamwork, organizations can be afflicted with misdirected competitiveness, individualism ("what's in it for me?"), over-inflated egos, personal ambition and interpersonal conflicts. This detracts from an organization's ability to accomplish its objectives productively and economically.

The broken squares game demonstrates the essence of the collaborative value by illustrating how all the people in the organization belong to the same team. When collaboration is optimized, departments are not competing with one another but are linked. Recognition comes from how well the company meets its overall objectives, not from how well an individual or department performs. Teamwork means understanding that each victory spells success for the whole company.

senn delaney
the culture-shaping firm

HEIDRICK & STRUGGLES   © 1994-2017 Senn Delaney Leadership Consulting Group, LLC. All rights reserved.

the change value
innovation, feedback and coaching

> "The sure path to oblivion is to stay where you are."[14]

> Bernard Fauber

When a culture is operating in a healthy, high-performance state, new ideas, innovation and openness to change are typical. Lines of communication are open and people are willing to accept different points of view—the culture is virtually free of "destructive criticism."

When an organization is deficient in the change value, its results will suffer. Employees in the organization tend to view both change and new ideas through what we describe as Observer/Critic/Judge eyes (see Chapter 9, "Change"). In this type of culture, innovation and agility are stifled.

The "Bizarro" cartoons by Dan Piraro are reprinted by permission
of Chronicle Features, San Francisco, California ©1990

Change embodies agility and resilience. People and companies that will be winners in the years ahead will be those that are more agile and adaptable. As the game changes, they will rapidly adjust the new conditions and recover more quickly after setbacks and temporary defeats. They will have a better ability to bounce back and remain hopeful and optimistic in the face of adversity.

Another aspect of change is individual and organizational learning. A culture that is strong in the change value will support individual learning and foster its employees' personal commitments to learn and grow. It will also harbor an organizational commitment to employee development, feedback and coaching.

© 1994-2017 Senn Delaney Leadership Consulting Group, LLC. All rights reserved.

HEIDRICK & STRUGGLES

the ethics/integrity value
the essential bottom line

"There is no right way to do a wrong thing."[15]

Kenneth Blanchard and
Norman Vincent Peale

"Stan, are you walking off with my
'Ethics in the Workplace' book?"

www.cartoonresource.com

Ethics and integrity are core foundational values. Without them, there is no foundation for trust between people, or between companies and customers or stakeholders. Integrity implies a wholeness or congruence between words and deeds. When integrity is present, people are living the message or "walking the talk."

A commitment to ethics suggests a higher order: that people look beyond themselves to the greater good when making decisions. Ethics can be loosely defined as a system of moral standards that individuals and organizations use to guide decisions and daily behaviors. This was something that was once taken for granted. The rash of ethical violations by dozens of well-known companies in the recent past has put added focus back on this important value.

After years of working in organizations and listening to thousands of leaders, it seems that the most common elements of ethics and integrity are:

■ Honesty

■ Trustworthiness

■ Fairness

■ Mutual respect

■ Compassion

■ Social responsibility

senn delaney
the culture-shaping firm

HEIDRICK & STRUGGLES

© 1994-2017 Senn Delaney Leadership Consulting Group, LLC. All rights reserved.

the organizational health value

> "The power that comes from the high-quality thinking of an organization
> that is up on the Mood Elevator is hard to beat."

Larry Senn, Chairman, Senn Delaney

Organizational climate, or organizational health, is the most overlooked and underappreciated of all the essential values. The quality of organizational health can be gauged in much the same way as individual health on the Mood Elevator. When individuals, teams and organizations are at their best, they display the characteristics in the upper ranges: cooperation, flexibility, patience, appreciation, creativity, insight, generosity and gratitude.

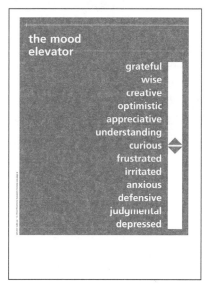

Organizations at lower levels of organizational health are more judgmental, stressed out, burned out, mistrusting, self-centered and negative. The implications of poor organizational health on both people and performance are enormous. A low level of organizational health creates unwanted turnover, impedes customer service, undermines quality initiatives and leads to victim behavior and hidden agendas. When hidden agendas build and trust is broken between individuals or teams, it becomes much more difficult to get things done.

In healthy environments, just the opposite is true: employee retention, customer service, quality and accountability are prevalent. Healthy organizations foster openness and trust; employees are encouraged to voice their point of view and to challenge old ways of doing things; and innovation becomes the norm. This type of candid and open environment creates better results, a better place to work and more success for individuals and the organization alike.

the customer value: purpose

Organizations and people operate in healthier ways when they focus on a greater purpose: something beyond themselves. A truly outwardly-focused organization gets in its own way less often.

Rather than fight over turf, they collaborate to serve the end user. Rather than resist change, they embrace change that better satisfies their customers.

© 1994-2017 Senn Delaney Leadership Consulting Group, LLC. All rights reserved.

HEIDRICK & STRUGGLES

A useful cultural question to ask is, "Are we inwardly focused and caught up in internal issues, or are we outwardly focused on serving our customer?" A customer-centric organization makes the customer an explicit part of their vision, mission and/or values.

creating values that live versus those that hang on the wall

Even though most organizations have established value sets, the majority still fall short of having an ideal culture. What creates this shortfall?

One contributor is having an incomplete value set. When many organizations think of values, they think of the foundational values like ethics, integrity, trust and respect. While these are critical, by themselves they will not create a healthy, high-performance culture. Few organizations we've encountered have considered values in their broader sense to include the entire Essential Value Set we've described above. Therefore, their cultural definition is insufficient.

Even having a complete set of values—one that incorporates all of the essential values—will not guarantee a healthy, high-performance organization. Simply writing down some values and sending them out in a memo to employees will not shape the culture. For the values to be ingrained in the culture, they must be the cornerstone of a comprehensive culture-shaping process.

The next chapter describes the importance of culture and a proven model for shaping it.

summary

As we mentioned in the first chapter, studies in corporate culture have found that the most critical common element of all successful organizations is that they use shared values more than policies and procedures as a means to guide employees in determining appropriate decisions and behaviors. The values help clarify those "grey areas" that aren't always covered by the rulebook.

Our research and experience has shown that the most successful individuals, teams and organizations place an equal focus on these six Essential Values:

- **Performance:** accountability and empowerment
- **Collaboration:** teamwork and mutual support
- **Change:** innovation, feedback and coaching
- **Ethics/Integrity:** honesty, fairness and social responsibility
- **Organizational Health:** operating "At Your Best"
- **Customer:** outward focus on a greater purpose

When each of these values plays an equal role in a larger culture-shaping effort, the result is greater long-term success.

HEIDRICK & STRUGGLES   © 1994-2017 Senn Delaney Leadership Consulting Group, LLC. All rights reserved.

questions, action steps and assignments

In this chapter, we talk about the critical role values play in shaping a culture. We urge you to reflect upon the following questions as you think about the values in your own culture.

1. What stated or unstated values of your organization are alive and well?

_____

_____

_____

_____

2. Which of the Essential Values are the people in your organization most successful in following and which ones seem the most difficult?

_____

_____

_____

_____

3. How do the Essential Values fit with your own set of personal values?

_____

_____

_____

_____

4. What culture barriers or counter-productive habits do you see in the organization?

_____

_____

_____

_____

5. Which of the Essential Values are not explicit or clear in your organization's value set?

_____

_____

_____

_____

© 1994-2017 Senn Delaney Leadership Consulting Group, LLC. All rights reserved.

HEIDRICK & STRUGGLES   © 1994-2017 Senn Delaney Leadership Consulting Group, LLC. All rights reserved.

6

building a
winning culture

It is hard to find a business publication today that does not point out the impact of culture. Many, if not most, failures or shortfalls in mergers and acquisitions are due to culture. The reason most strategies or initiatives fail is the culture. The demise of many once highly-regarded companies can be traced to their leaders not living the right values. Many books have pointed out the role of culture in successful organizations.

While it has been discussed and studied for years, culture is a relatively new concept in the history of business management. Corporate culture was first introduced in the academic and research community by Larry Senn in 1969, in his doctoral dissertation entitled *Organizational Character as a Methodological Tool in the Analysis of Business Organizations*. It wasn't until nine years later that Allan A. Kennedy and Terrence E. Deal popularized the term "corporate culture" in their book, *Corporate Cultures: The Rites and Rituals of Corporate Life*. Organizational culture further became popularized through two books published in early 80's: *The Art of Japanese Management*[16] by Tony Athos and Richard T. Pascale, and the best-selling *In Search of Excellence* by Thomas J. Peters and Robert H. Waterman (which we referred to in the first chapter). In recent years, John Kotter of Harvard University has done much to demonstrate the power of culture. His book *Corporate Culture and Performance*[17] tracks companies over a decade and shows that those with a strong and healthy culture outperformed others by a wide margin.

Throughout this time, Senn Delaney has gained decades of hands-on experience in corporate culture shaping. We have measurably reshaped the cultures of hundreds of organizations and teams, transforming them into energetic, high-performance work environments. We have accomplished this through the comprehensive, time-tested culture-shaping approach described in this chapter.

what is culture?

Corporate culture is similar to the personality of an individual. It is the more subjective, invisible side of the organization that determines the ways in which the company goes about its daily business.

Culture has been described as:

- The way we do things around here
- The norms and habits of the organization

© 1994-2017 Senn Delaney Leadership Consulting Group, LLC. All rights reserved.

HEIDRICK & STRUGGLES

In an organization with a strong culture, you can actually feel the human energy that flows from aligned, committed employees. In an organization with a weak or unaligned culture, the available human energy is fragmented and often dissipated through conflict, blaming and unclear communication. To the leaders of a company, corporate culture represents a powerful force, which, with proper attention and leadership, can be harnessed and managed for the good of the company and its employees.

strategy, structure and culture

Senn Delaney has developed a simplified version of the 7-S Model: **the Strategy-Structure-Culture Model**.

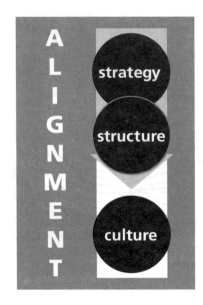

Based on over 25 years of experience, we've learned that the most successful organizations have:

- Clarity about their direction, strategy and strategic imperatives
- The appropriate organizational model or structure, together with effective systems and processes
- A healthy, high-performance culture

When all three of these are aligned, appropriate and mutually supportive, success is almost guaranteed.

However, this is usually not the case. During turbulent times, organizations consciously and systematically respond by implementing new strategies, systems, processes and structures. Rarely do they address the human engine that will drive these changes: the culture.

senn delaney
the culture-shaping firm

HEIDRICK & STRUGGLES

© 1994-2017 Senn Delaney Leadership Consulting Group, LLC. All rights reserved.

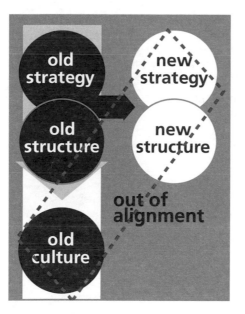

The result of this misalignment is that the organization now finds itself unable to successfully respond to and implement new strategies with the old culture. This results in high levels of stress, burnout and tension as people push harder and harder. The net impact of the organizational mis-alignment is that the internal cultural problems tend to interfere with the organization's competitive abilities, and the results and performance of the business suffer.

a culture-shaping model

There is a science to shaping a culture: a set of principles and steps, which when followed, will almost always ensure measurable change in the behaviors of organizations. It is a five-step model that starts by understanding the current culture and defining the desired culture. The other four elements include training to "unfreeze" old, dysfunctional behaviors, implementing a system to rein-force new behaviors, focusing the new behaviors on business applications, and measuring results.

Integrated approach needed to shape team behaviors and the culture

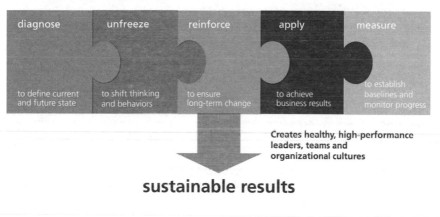

diagnose	unfreeze	reinforce	apply	measure
to define current and future state	to shift thinking and behaviors	to ensure long-term change	to achieve business results	to establish baselines and monitor progress

Creates healthy, high-performance leaders, teams and organizational cultures

sustainable results

© 1994-2017 Senn Delaney Leadership Consulting Group, LLC. All rights reserved.

senn delaney
the culture-shaping firm

HEIDRICK & STRUGGLES

Understand the Current Culture and Define Desired Culture

One of the primary reasons the majority of leaders fail to address the culture of their organization is because of a phenomenon called **familiarity blindness**. Familiarity blindness occurs when a person can no longer recognize the difference between the culture they work in and the rest of the world. It's much like living in Los Angeles too long and no longer noticing the smog, or in New York City and becoming less aware of the noise.

There's an old saying about this: *"We don't know who discovered water, but we know it wasn't the fish."*

Drawing by P. Kleba; ©1994, SDLCG.

Understanding your culture is a similar phenomenon. It's like water to a fish. We are surrounded by it every day, and unless we take an objective look, we will not be able to see it. The first step to understanding your culture is to observe your organization objectively, as if you were an outsider.

In addition, it is useful to get feedback from people at different levels in the organization. Ask new employees to describe the culture, the values and the personality of the company (or of the department if you are focusing on that level). A convenient assessment tool we use at Senn Delaney is the Corporate Culture Profile™, which measures several different dimensions of a team against the Essential Value Set. You may have seen the results in your culture-shaping session. We based the questions on our years of studying the cultural characteristics in hundreds of organizations that contribute to or detract from their performance.

Once you have an understanding of your current culture, you must define how the culture needs to be in order to reach your goals. In the previous chapter, we discussed how to shape your culture through values and described the Essential Value Set needed.

Unfreeze Old Behaviors and Internalize Desired Behaviors

Organizational and individual habits can either support or undermine a healthy, high-performance culture. Our personal behaviors come from lifelong habits, which are based on underlying beliefs and thinking. An organizational culture is a collection of individual behavioral habits that a group of people has developed over time.

Most existing dysfunctions in organizational cultures are learned habits like "we-they" games. For the culture to shift, these habits must shift.

As you saw in the session, people learn best by experiencing. The insight-based learning you've experienced is the best way we have found to help people recognize the habits that may be causing their dysfunctional behaviors and connect to more effective thinking that will drive more effective behaviors.

HEIDRICK & STRUGGLES

© 1994-2017 Senn Delaney Leadership Consulting Group, LLC. All rights reserved.

The best way to live the values is to gain an understanding, awareness and accountability for the thinking that drives our behaviors. Learning more about how our quality of thinking affects our behavior is the most important part of the educational process you are going through.

In order to shape a culture, a critical mass of people must take part in an unfreezing experience such as the one you had.

Reinforcement

Once a person gains new insights and begins to see the world differently, it is critical to have consistent and frequent reinforcement to ensure the behavior change becomes a way of life. That's why reinforcement is such an important part of the culture-shaping process.

There are three aspects to culture-shaping reinforcement. One is through the more formal systems, which need to be supportive of the values and guiding behaviors: Procedures such as hiring new employees, orientation, performance management, or 360° assessments should all explicitly incorporate the values.

The second aspect of culture-shaping reinforcement is informal reinforcement, which primarily takes the form of coaching and feedback. Shaping a healthy, high-performance culture requires a feedback-rich environment. The most powerful tool you can use for informally reinforcing the new and desired behaviors is providing positive reinforcement for your employees. The practice of catching people doing things right, and recognizing them specifically for the desired behavior, is a great way to help people develop positive new habits. While many people see this type of "cash and carry coaching" as a tool for correcting or improving performance, we believe that in order to shape a healthy culture you must give feedback on how people are living the values as well.

It is useful to build into your organization a way for people to offer feedback to one another on the values. Everyone in the organization, especially the managers, needs a way to receive feedback on which values they represent well and which ones they need to work on. When a culture is operating in a healthy, high-performance state, employees will not only be role models of the values, they will also proactively solicit feedback from others.

The third aspect of culture-shaping reinforcement is consistent periodical reminders of the insights and concepts learned as a result of the unfreezing process. Throughout your engagement in the culture-shaping process, you will receive periodic e-mails through our eCoach® system to help you do this. You and your teammates may come up with other ways as well.

Application

The purpose of a high-performance culture is to create both results and a healthier organization. Therefore the best way to bring the values alive is to use them day-to-day in executing strategies and achieving goals. This should take place on an individual, team and organization-wide level. If individuals are accountable, if teams work together effectively to make decisions and take action, and if initiatives can be implemented collaboratively throughout the organization, then improved results will follow.

Ideally, you experienced the session as a part of an intact work team, so you can use the concepts in your meetings or in dealing with your teammates over various business issues.

Measurement

People pay attention to what is measured, so if you want to improve something, measure it. The feedback from measurement prompts action.

senn delaney
the culture-shaping firm

© 1994-2017 Senn Delaney Leadership Consulting Group, LLC. All rights reserved.

HEIDRICK & STRUGGLES

At the individual level, employees can be effectively measured using a Guiding Behaviors Inventory™. This is a specialized form of peer and direct report feedback much like a 360° survey, but tailored to the specific values and guiding behaviors of your organization.

Your team or organization can periodically repeat the Corporate Culture Profile™ process to see how you are progressing.

Role-Modeling—Shadow of the Leader

Culture shaping is a leader-led process. The model described here works best when it begins with the key leaders. Their ability to live the values will be a direct predictor of whether the rest of the organization will live them as well.

Over time, organizations take on the characteristics of the leaders; therefore, leaders from the top down need to commit to living the values in order to shape the culture. This is where integrity is critical. If you and your team are unable to be exemplary role models of the values, then the people who work for you will have permission to behave the same way—they will feel that they do not have to live them either.

If there are leaders that clearly do not support the values, people will wonder if culture change is another "flavor of the day." They will ask, "How committed are we to these new behaviors? Does it really matter if everyone doesn't get on board?" For a cultural transformation to be successful, the organizational leadership must be willing to confront and coach those people who seem unable or unwilling to be part of the new culture, and ask them to resign if no progress is made.

connecting culture and strategy

The purpose of a high-performance culture is to better execute strategies in order to improve business results. It is often helpful for people in a firm to have a simple graphical way to see this connection.

The High-Performance Pyramid

One way we have done that with our clients is to help them construct a high-performance pyramid to align the senior team around the elements shown in the figure below.

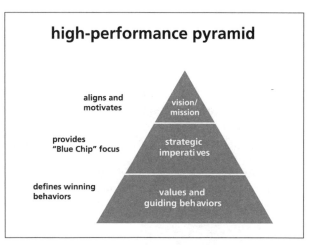

HEIDRICK & STRUGGLES   © 1994-2017 Senn Delaney Leadership Consulting Group, LLC. All rights reserved.

summary

Cultures can be systematically shaped to better support business results and to make companies great places to work. A leader's most important mission is to set a clear direction and role model the healthy, high-performance behaviors needed to make it happen.

This chapter has described a process many others have used to measurably shift elements in the culture. It does take determination, persistence and a commitment to personal change. Leaders must be sensitive to the messages their day-to-day and even minute-to-minute behaviors send to the organization.

> "Until most everyone lives the values, the full potential of the culture will not be realized. So in a truly healthy, high-performance culture, every team player at every level is also a leader by fully taking responsibility for his or her own behaviors, and living the shared values of the organization."[18]

Larry Senn, 21st Century Leadership

© 1994-2017 Senn Delaney Leadership Consulting Group, LLC. All rights reserved.

questions, action steps and assignments

1. Try to look at your organization with a "stranger's eyes." What are the strengths you see or feel in the culture?

   _____

   _____

   _____

   _____

2. List at least one obvious cultural barrier.

   _____

   _____

   _____

   _____

3. Think of a key strategic initiative or imperative of your own function or group. What is it about the culture that will help that initiative succeed?

   _____

   _____

   _____

   _____

4. What is the most obvious cultural barrier that will get in the way?

   _____

   _____

   _____

HEIDRICK & STRUGGLES

© 1994-2017 Senn Delaney Leadership Consulting Group, LLC. All rights reserved.

7

accountability

accountability: the performance value

Georgette Mosbacher, a successful business owner and author, was asked how she climbed from poverty and obscurity to the very highest levels of success. She replied, "I know I can't be a **winner** and a **whiner** at the same time. And I'm a **winner**."[19]

Barbara Levy Kipper, chairman of Charles Levy Company, discusses the importance of empowerment in this comment:

> "Empowered people believe that they can make significant change in the world around them. When you have that philosophy, there is nothing that cannot be done."[20]

Accountability and empowerment go hand-in-hand. People who feel accountable for the results of their own actions and behaviors tend to have more control over those results. They are more empowered to make a difference in their own circumstances and those of others. For this reason, accountability is a cornerstone for most successful people and organizations.

"don't blame me"

In contrast, the book *A Nation of Victims* by Charles J. Sykes points to the decline in American competitiveness, as well as erosion of our quality of life, due to a general feeling of lack of control, a sense of having no power over events or circumstances. Sykes refers to this as "the victimization of America."

Sykes sums up the answer to this trend in the following quote:

> "Recognizing our own responsibility and the need to stop blaming others is the first step toward dismantling the culture of victimization."[21]

© 1994-2017 Senn Delaney Leadership Consulting Group, LLC. All rights reserved.

HEIDRICK & STRUGGLES

From The Wall Street Journal—Permission, Cartoon Features Syndicate.

Victim attitudes abound in many organizations. These attitudes manifest in such behavior as blaming, excuses, defensive maneuvers and statements like, "it's not my job," "it's his/her fault," or "it's not our policy." People often use statements such as these as a shield against taking risks and accepting their own personal accountability. This can directly affect productivity, efficiency and the bottom line.

We know accountable attitudes must exist somewhere within every organization, otherwise nothing would ever get accomplished. So how do we create more accountability and less victim behavior?

As we discussed in previous chapters, and in the Senn Delaney culture-shaping session, our behavior is a result of our thinking, or state of mind.

accountability as a state of mind

> Mary expected to be vice-president in five years; ten years later she is still a mid-level manager.

> Gary dreamed of being an artist in Paris and wound up teaching high school drama.

> Susan wanted to be a ballerina but a car accident crushed her knee and now she is a computer programmer.

> Phil expected to get married, take care of his family, and live happily ever after. He has two kids who need braces, he lost his job, and he and his wife have problems with their relationship.

At times, the results we get are not the results we expected. It happens to all of us, yet some people feel victimized by the events and circumstances of their lives, while others always seem to make the best of whatever happens. The difference between victims and victors is their point of view.

People with a point of view of personal accountability tend to look for what they might learn from any given situation. If something isn't working out, they ask themselves, "How can I prevent this from happening in the future?" They look first at their own actions, asking such questions as:

- What clues did I not see?

- What extra steps could I have taken?

- What opportunities did I miss by being unwilling to take risks?

- Whom (or what) did I fail to confront soon enough?

- What lessons could I have learned sooner to avoid this?

senn delaney
the culture-shaping firm

HEIDRICK & STRUGGLES   © 1994-2017 Senn Delaney Leadership Consulting Group, LLC. All rights reserved.

- What personality traits or habits of mine might have aggravated the situation?
- What more can I do to create the results?

the accountability ladder

The following is the Accountability Ladder, which can help you determine your personal level of accountability.

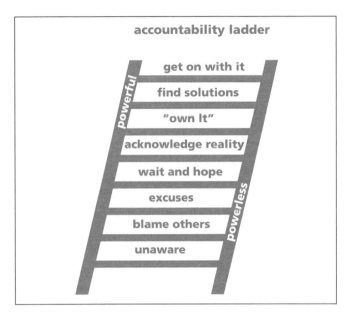

The lower levels of accountability are marked by a feeling of helplessness and lack of power, while higher levels reflect an attitude of "what more can I do?"

The upper levels of accountability are characterized by action orientation, a desire to "make a difference," a willingness to learn and an honest search for personal improvement opportunities. At these higher levels, there is generally a feeling of empowerment, self-confidence and a sense of personal security.

accountability and quality of thought

To operate at the highest levels of personal accountability, it is critical that we begin to become more aware of the thinking that precedes both victim and accountable behavior.

The thinking that precedes victim behavior includes thoughts like, "Why me? How did this happen to me?" or sometimes, "Who did this to me?" At lower levels of accountability, the thinking is that "life is not fair." People at these levels react to life's unfairness by getting angry and blaming others. They often feel that circumstances and events are out of control.

The thinking that precedes accountable behavior includes thoughts like, "Okay, what do I do now? What is there to learn from this?" Higher levels of accountability yield better results as people take accountability for their actions and have more control over the outcome. By eliminating blame and the focus on the errors of others, many causes of interpersonal conflict are eliminated, resulting in better relationships.

© 1994-2017 Senn Delaney Leadership Consulting Group, LLC. All rights reserved.

HEIDRICK & STRUGGLES

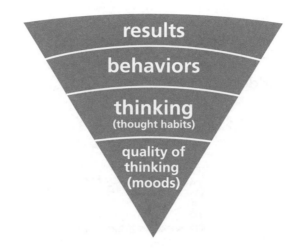

Of course, it is not humanly possible to operate at the highest level of accountability in every minute of every day. The reality is that at times we all become caught up in low-quality thinking; we all at times lose our perspective. What should we do if when we're stuck in low-quality thinking and contemplating victim behavior?

First, be aware of what is occurring. Remember, your clues are your moods and feelings. Feelings such as powerlessness, anger, resentment and desire to blame are clear indicators that your thinking is not of great quality.

Second, acknowledge that you are caught up in victim thinking. Understand that your thinking is not reliable and may result in low-quality behavior if you aren't cautious. Delay action or making decisions if at all possible. Wait until your perspective shifts a bit, as evidenced by more feelings of calm, acceptance and hope.

If you're not able to delay action, get someone else's coaching; preferably someone who will be objective and help you to see some good options. Don't look for someone who will commiserate with you and shower you with sympathy. Instead, look for someone who will shower you with a dose of perspective.

Third, remember that low moods and low-quality thinking are temporary. Even though it may not feel like it, this, too, shall pass.

the role of choice in accountability

Everyone can act accountably at times and feel like a victim at others. When we are operating from higher-quality thinking, accountability tends to be our natural default setting. On the other hand, when we are experiencing lower-quality thinking, the role of personal choice becomes critical.

Throughout the process of striving towards a particular result, there will always be opportunities for personal choice, if we recognize them.

When we are feeling victimized, it feels like our choices are very limited. We feel powerless. We may find ourselves blaming others or making excuses about the outcome.

As we become more aware of the impact of our thinking, via our moods, or "the way we feel," we can catch ourselves before we automatically act on our lower-quality thinking. We can see our situation with more perspective, and that we do have a choice of actions that can help us influence the outcome we want.

HEIDRICK & STRUGGLES   © 1994-2017 Senn Delaney Leadership Consulting Group, LLC. All rights reserved.

Even when we do all we can to get the desired results and are not successful, we still have a choice: we can choose to learn, or not to learn, for the future; to either accept the outcome with grace and humility, or to feel resentful and angry.

Making a choice to be accountable is like choosing between two pairs of glasses. One pair of glasses magnifies the way we were victimized. "Others did not do what they said they would; another person made a mistake; Department B missed its deadline."

The other set of glasses will magnify the accountable things we could have done. "I could have involved more people to ensure the success of this project; the other person's mistake could have easily been corrected if I had followed up in time; my communication to department B was not as clear as it should have been." This set of glasses keeps the spotlight focused in a healthy way on our own actions and choices rather than the actions and choices of others. That way, we learn what we can do better next time.

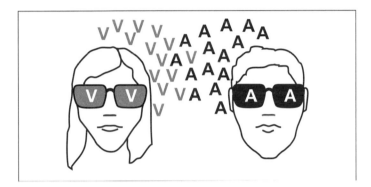

the value of accountability:
understanding the payoffs and prices

We do not always understand the tremendous life-enhancing benefits or payoffs we get from being accountable. These payoffs include:

- Learning and growing from mistakes
- Focusing on solutions with a "can-do" attitude
- Getting more results
- Being more in control of our lives
- Gaining more respect from others
- Having higher self-esteem

Naturally, there are prices we pay to behave accountably, especially when we fall short of a desired outcome. We have to:

- Admit we made a mistake or contributed to the shortfall
- Assume some risk (if it is culturally not okay to make a mistake)
- Look imperfect
- Take on more work to fix it

© 1994-2017 Senn Delaney Leadership Consulting Group, LLC. All rights reserved.

What do you notice about the prices we pay for being accountable? They are usually momentary ones, or **short-term** in nature. Now look at the list of payoffs: learning, growing, getting better results and feeling more control of our lives. These benefits are clearly **long-term** in nature.

Given the powerful long-term benefits of being accountable, why do we hear excuses, blaming and finger pointing? There must be payoffs or perceived benefits from looking at life as a victim and then sharing those experiences with others. Some of the payoffs of being a victim might be:

- Gaining sympathy

- Avoiding blame—it isn't my fault

- Saving face (ego)

- Holding on to an erroneous belief—"I'm right; I don't make mistakes"

- Avoiding the risk of making a mistake

- Avoiding work—"I can't change the outcome anyway…"

There are also prices to pay when one plays the victim, especially if it becomes a habit or lifestyle choice. The prices include:

- Fewer results

- Not learning from, and therefore repeating, our mistakes

- Not growing from experiences

- Loss of respect from others

- Loss of self-respect

- A feeling of powerlessness

- Less control of our lives

In contrast to the **long-term** benefits of accountability, payoffs from a victim attitude are short-term in nature. To get **short-term** relief, like sympathy, we pay the long-term price of getting stuck where we are, without learning or growing, and being less in control of our lives.

serenity and "gravity"

Is it possible to be accountable for everything in our life? Are there not, in fact, things over which we have no control?

Of course there are. So how do we take on an accountable point of view when we are faced with a situation that is clearly beyond our control?

The answer to this question lies in the Serenity Prayer, attributed to American theologian Reinhold Niebuhr.

> Grant me the serenity to accept the things I cannot change, the courage to change the things I can, and the wisdom to know the difference.

HEIDRICK & STRUGGLES   © 1994-2017 Senn Delaney Leadership Consulting Group, LLC. All rights reserved.

We refer to the "things I cannot change" as gravity issues. They are those things, like the force of gravity, which affect us but we are powerless to change. There certainly are many of those things in the business world; we often tend to waste a lot of time and energy on them, mostly by complaining or wishing things were different.

Some examples of gravity issues are:

- Corporate governance
- Government regulations
- Store locations
- The weather
- The economy
- Our boss
- Mergers, acquisitions, consolidation
- Too much to do in too little time

When it comes to gravity, perhaps this bull's-eye of issues may remind you of where to place your time, energy and focus.

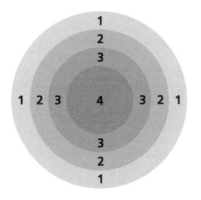

1. Things outside of my control, where I do not have input—gravity issues
2. Things outside of my control where I can give input and move on
3. Things I can influence
4. Things I can impact directly (spend most time and energy here)

Learning to accept gravity issues is an important life-effectiveness principle. As long as we spend most of our time and energy towards the center of the bulls-eye, i.e., "things I can impact directly," or "things I can influence," then we are moving in a positive direction. Once we feel we've done everything we can and the situation still does not meet our expectations, then we have a choice: keep trying, or accept it and move on.

"The wisdom to know the difference" is where each person decides to draw the line, where each decides "that is all I am going to do right now." Once we have done all we can and make a decision to put something in the category of "things I cannot change," truly accept it and let it go, the result is a feeling of serenity. We gain peace of mind, access to greater creativity, and the energy to be productive in other endeavors.

© 1994-2017 Senn Delaney Leadership Consulting Group, LLC. All rights reserved.

Calvin and Hobbes ©1994; Watterson. Reprinted with permission of Universal Press Syndicate. All rights reserved.

Accepting the situation does not mean that you condone the behavior or the outcome. Rather, acceptance and humility releases resilience and energy to continue through the demands of the day, and to gain the perspective necessary to choose the right path.

accountability versus responsibility

People often ask the difference between **accountability** and **responsibility**. While there is a large overlap between these two concepts, here is one way to distinguish between the two:

Responsibility pertains to identified tasks.

Accountability is a self-empowered mindset.

A data entry operator might be responsible for entering information correctly into a computer system. A personally accountable data entry operator would look for ways to make the entire system more effective. A supervisor takes responsibility for departmental operations, but his/her accountability is to the mission and goals of the entire organization, as well as the department and the work group.

Another way to look at it is: Responsibility is the task that I have agreed to perform. Accountability is the manner in which I carry out that task.

We've differentiated the two in the following illustration:

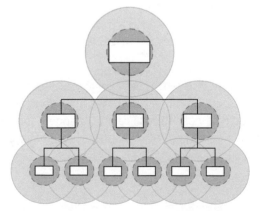

senn delaney
the culture-shaping firm

HEIDRICK & STRUGGLES

© 1994-2017 Senn Delaney Leadership Consulting Group, LLC. All rights reserved.

The dotted circles represent what I am responsible for. However, what I take accountability for is much broader, as represented by the light circles. With an attitude of accountability, things are less likely to "fall through the cracks." Much like the Broken Squares game, finishing my own square is being responsible; working together to finish all the squares is being accountable.

creating more accountability in the workplace

"In my experience, this one trait—accountability, more than any other, can make the difference in a company or a person being a moderate performer or an excellent one."

Larry Senn, Chairman, Senn Delaney

How can you contribute to greater accountability in those around you? Here are three ways that have proven extremely effective in creating accountable teams and organizations.

Become Aware of Levels of Accountability

Making excuses and blaming others for errors or lack of results is an unconscious habit in many organizations. It is like the air we breathe; we are so used to it we often do not notice it. Therefore, the first step in creating more accountability is awareness. Be aware that the quality of our thinking, and therefore the level of our perspective and ability to be accountable, fluctuates. This happens to all of us. Sometimes we have perspective where accountability is natural and easy and sometimes we don't. The key is to be aware of where we are. The biggest clue, as we discussed earlier, is our feelings.

An organizational version of the Accountability Ladder is the Business Accountability Chart. It reinforces the learning from the Broken Squares game and helps people identify how big a team they are willing to play on.

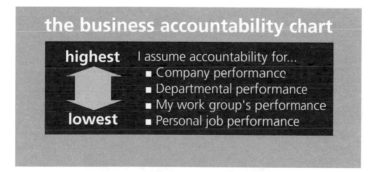

Here are several comments that reflect different degrees of accountability:

High Levels of Accountability

- What else can we do to make sure this works?
- Let's work together to get this done.
- It was my mistake. Here's what I plan to do now.
- Let's learn from this and do it differently next time.
- Let's make sure all the bases are covered and that we haven't forgotten anything.
- Who might have some fresh ideas?

© 1994-2017 Senn Delaney Leadership Consulting Group, LLC. All rights reserved.

Low Levels of Accountability

- It's not my department!

- It's not our fault we didn't make the deadline; engineering didn't do their job; the ads are lousy; we didn't have enough lead-time; etc.

- I can't do this, corporate won't sign off on the equipment that I need.

- What's in it for me?

- I can't manage these people; they don't want to work.

- My hands are tied; it's against policy; we never do it that way.

"You'll notice my grades reflect the shocking ineptitude of the school system."

Drawing by Capelini; ©1993 The Saturday Evening Post

Role-Model Accountability

The second step is to be a model of accountability yourself. Once you are aware of accountability it is easier to role model it for others. This is important since it is hard to create accountability without an example. Actions speak louder than words.

Be aware when you are casting an accountable shadow as well as when you are not. Casting an accountable shadow means you acknowledge when you have missed a goal and don't blame others or make excuses. Use your moods and feelings as the barometer of the quality of your thinking. Be cautious when your mood is down and the quality of your thinking is low. It is easy to fall into victim attitudes and behavior in that state. Remember the benefits of an accountable mindset.

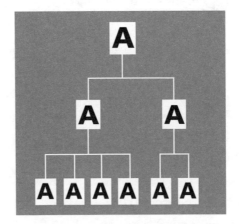

HEIDRICK & STRUGGLES   © 1994-2017 Senn Delaney Leadership Consulting Group, LLC. All rights reserved.

Help Others Be More Accountable

The more you realize that lack of accountability comes from low-quality thinking and that everyone experiences this at times, the more effective you will be in working with those caught up in victim thinking and behavior. Understanding that they are temporarily "lost" in their unreliable thinking will enable you to approach them with some compassion. It is important that you don't ignore their ineffective behavior and results, but when you do interact with them, begin with an attitude of understanding and then respectfully discuss their behavior and results by following these two steps:

■ Listen and respectfully acknowledge the obstacles they may have faced.

■ Ask how you can help them achieve your mutual objectives. The key phrase is, "What more can we do to get the results?"

summary

Tiger ©1976; Reprinted with special permission of King Features Syndicate.

How much time is wasted daily in your organization on "arguing about what went wrong on the last play"? Victim behaviors such as blaming and making excuses, and attitudes like "it's not my job" are evident in organizations everywhere.

Creating an accountable organization begins within each one of us. Accountability is a state of mind or point of view that we are in control of our own destiny, rather than victims of circumstance. People with this point of view tend to look for what they might learn from a situation and take a proactive stance to influence the future. They waste little time complaining or worrying about gravity issues, or things they can't control, and instead direct their energy towards the things they can control or influence.

Accountable people ask themselves:

What more can I do to get the results?

© 1994–2017 Senn Delaney Leadership Consulting Group, LLC. All rights reserved

senn delaney
the culture-shaping firm

HEIDRICK & STRUGGLES

questions, action steps and assignments

1. Think of a success in your life; something you feel proud of. It could be a success at work, at home, in your community, at school or with friends or family. Reflect for a moment on how you approached this project. What were some obstacles you encountered? What attitudes did you hold? How did you feel? What helped you reach your objectives?

_____

_____

_____

_____

_____

2. Now think of an example where you did not experience the success you expected. How did you approach this project? What attitudes did you hold? How did they differ from the successful example above?

_____

_____

_____

_____

_____

3. What issues do people around you spend time worrying about or blaming others for—issues where they feel somewhat victimized? Are these gravity issues? If not, create an action plan for moving those people up to a higher level of accountability.

_____

_____

_____

_____

_____

4. Which group inside or outside the company does your group normally blame? In what way is your organization accountable for the problem? What can you do the change the outcome?

_____

_____

_____

_____

_____

senn delaney
the culture-shaping firm

HEIDRICK & STRUGGLES

© 1994-2017 Senn Delaney Leadership Consulting Group, LLC. All rights reserved.

8

teamwork

teamwork:

the collaborative value

In the past, many organizations paid lip service to such factors as teamwork, organizational values and culture, but seldom addressed them as corporate priorities. This is primarily because it was less obvious how these "soft" factors contributed to the bottom line.

In the 21st century, with its chaotic environment of global competition and rapid technological innovation, change has become a way of life; and more and more organizations have realized the necessity of good teamwork. The growing acceptance of quality improvement programs and shared service organizations having to do "more with less" has created an environment where leaders and managers are increasingly aware of the need to develop effective teams. Today, many leading-edge corporations have proven that teamwork does impact the bottom line—often dramatically. Teamwork is not just "nice to have," it is a "must-have."

"In our present time, we must begin to celebrate collective entrepreneurship," says Robert Reich, former U.S. secretary of labor, in an article describing how the team, not the individual, is the corporate champion. To make our corporate systems work, he says, we need "endeavors in which the whole of the effort is greater than the sum of individual contributions. We need to honor our teams more, our aggressive leaders and maverick geniuses less."[22]

Many business experts now believe that the ability to develop and lead good teams is the number one skill required to be a high-performing leader in today's organizations. Downsizing, outsourcing, reorganizing and retooling are all indications of the pressure on organizations to reduce the size of workforces. This often leaves departments and work groups with fewer people to do even more work. The only way to cope with this is by working together cooperatively in an environment of respect, and drawing on all the talent and resources available to get the job done.

> An effective team is a group of people acting together in an atmosphere of trust and accountability who agree that the best way to achieve a common goal is to cooperate.

© 1994-2017 Senn Delaney Leadership Consulting Group, LLC. All rights reserved.

what is teamwork?

Think about some of the teams of which you've been a part: maybe a committee, a department team, a project team or even a one-on-one effort. Perhaps it was in your personal life, in your family or on a sports or community team. Bring to mind a time when you were on a team where everything seemed to click. The results were great, you had strong rapport with the other members, there were creative solutions, and everyone participated and contributed. It was almost like the whole team was operating "in the zone." The collective synergy created by teams in this state allows them to reach goals above and beyond what their capabilities might normally be. You may have heard the expression "playing over their heads": This is a term used to describe teams that achieve a performance state beyond most people's expectations. This healthy, high-performance state is attainable by any team.

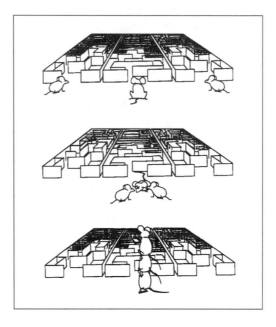

Building a team!

By permission of Southern California Association of Governments

benefits of good teamwork

When people work together in an atmosphere of trust and accountability toward a common goal, they are able to put aside turf issues and politics, and collectively focus on the task at hand. This focused application of resources allows organizations to break through barriers, identify new opportunities and create a momentum that leads to three major bottom-line benefits:

- Better problem-solving and innovation
- Greater productivity
- More effective use of resources

Jon R. Katzenbach is a renowned authority on teams, and co-author of *The Wisdom of Teams*. In answer to the question of why training teams are so popular, he says, "Because they produce extra performance results. There is virtually no environment in which teams—if done right—can't have a measurable impact on the performance of an organization."[23]

HEIDRICK & STRUGGLES   © 1994-2017 Senn Delaney Leadership Consulting Group, LLC. All rights reserved.

The benefits listed above are critical to the success of the organization. There are also many subjective benefits of teamwork that greatly enhance the working environment:

■ People enjoy working together; teamwork fills a need for socialization.

■ Working as part of a team helps people grow as they learn from each other and develop important skills in a safe environment.

■ Working together toward a common goal provides a sense of purpose that is motivating and fulfilling.

> "Rather than one leader, now we are going to have many leaders throughout organizations and society. In order for us to advance many leaders, everyone is going to have to advance. If someone is diminished, we're all diminished. There is a much greater sense of team, of 'we're all in this together, working toward something.' And when we create a high-functioning team, that's a very exciting and productive group."[24]
>
> Marjorie M. Blanchard, president of Blanchard Training and Development, Inc.

obstacles of teamwork

If it's so apparent that teamwork is important, why is it that creating a sustainable, collaborative culture seems to be so challenging to achieve and so difficult to maintain?

Drawing by P. Kleba; ©1994 SDLCG

Embedded in each organization's culture are some pervasive **thought habits** that hinder teamwork efforts. These thought habits revolve around the high value given to individual achievement.

In the article mentioned earlier in this chapter, economist Robert Reich explains how the "myth of individualism"[25] was instilled in our culture. In the early 1900's, popular author Horatio Alger penned a series of stories in which the hero was usually a poverty-stricken young man who became

© 1994-2017 Senn Delaney Leadership Consulting Group, LLC. All rights reserved.

HEIDRICK & STRUGGLES

a great success through a combination of hard work, perseverance and individual effort. This hero became the new paradigm for the culture of the times, a tradition that still exists today.

Although many organizations have embraced and espoused the value of teamwork, the cultures of most of these organizations still promote and reward individualism, tacitly encouraging individuals to compete for recognition, acknowledgement, attention and compensation. The strong focus on individual achievement in most cultures makes it difficult to establish commitment for the benefits of teamwork.

However, there are dozens of examples of teams that have achieved dramatic results by taking advantage of the "wisdom of the team."

Historical First: Groups Voluntarily Share Budget!

After extensive culture-shaping efforts, the senior team of a large telecommunications company got together for its annual meeting to complete the budget. For the first time in history, groups were willing to give up their budgeted dollars to other areas in order to move the organization forward.

GE's Plant Light Bill Cut In Half!

GE holds regular sessions where managers actively listen to the ideas of workers. This practice has resulted in innovations that have saved the company millions of dollars. One idea cut production time for a jet-combustion part by 90% and another cut the plant light bill in half! GE's collaborative environment is keeping it successful and competitive in today's rapidly changing global marketplace.

In *The Wisdom of Teams*, Jon R. Katzenbach and Douglas K. Smith offer proof of the critical relationship between collaboration and results:

> "The record of team performance speaks for itself…Motorola, recently acclaimed for surpassing its Japanese competition in producing the world's lightest, smallest and highest-quality cellular phones with only a few hundred parts versus over a thousand for the competition, relied heavily on teams to do it."[26]

We can see that the way to really get things done is through teamwork. We also know that it takes a shift in thinking to create a supportive culture and achieve a true breakthrough relative to an organization's commitment to teamwork.

Drawing by R. Morgan; ©1994 SDLCG

HEIDRICK & STRUGGLES

© 1994-2017 Senn Delaney Leadership Consulting Group, LLC. All rights reserved.

the broken squares game

The Broken Squares game played in the unfreezing session is a great metaphor for winning within an organization. If you have played it you will recall that individuals sit around tables in small groups with the challenge of each player assembling a square from puzzle pieces. In order to win the game, as defined in the rules, every person in the whole room has to complete their own square.

The unspoken goal, of course, is that people had to work together to make this occur. Some people felt like they "won" when they had completed their individual square. Many felt that the win occurred when their table had completed all their squares. But in truth, nobody won until everyone in the entire room had completed all the squares.

This analogy holds true for most organizations today. Can an individual win ensure the success or survival of an area or a department? Can a single area or department win ensure the success or survival of an organization? The old mentality of competition, protection of turf and hoarding of resources may result in an individual win, but this thinking often leads to organizational failure.

There is a need for more and better teamwork in all organizations. The broken squares game provides insights about how you play on a team. It can also show how, although we each have accountability for our own piece of the business, we also are connected together as an organization—it is the success of the entire organization that determines the whole win.

Here is what people have said about their insights into teamwork after their experience with the Broken Squares game:

> "In the Broken Squares game, I realized that I had trouble accepting help. At work my attitude is 'I'll solve the problem; just leave me alone and let me do my job. If you need some help, I'll be glad to help you out.' By taking the former attitude of 'Leave me alone,' I found that I did not allow other people to grow. In addition, I didn't allow them to add value that a lot of them could have added to the different projects.

> "I've learned to be quicker to ask people for help and not so protective of my own turf or domain."

> "While playing the Broken Squares game, I observed how some people got upset when they saw the solution to a puzzle that was very obvious to them but not the puzzle solver. I realized that I exhibit this same behavior at work. I get irritated when people can't 'solve the problem.' Instead of approaching people in a helpful way early, I let things build up, frustrated by the fact that they missed the obvious in their area of responsibility.

> "What an eye opener! Ever since then, I approach co-workers early and in a helpful way. It made a great deal of difference in my effectiveness and relationships with others."

Clues to Winning in the Game

Following are the clues called out during the game:

"Sometimes I must be willing to give the game away in order to win it."

"Rather than looking at what someone else can do, look at what you can do."

"Sometimes when I think I have my act together, I don't."

© 1994-2017 Senn Delaney Leadership Consulting Group, LLC. All rights reserved

"Sometimes I need to pause from the action and step back to view the bigger picture in order to see the obvious."

"Action produces results even when we don't know exactly what we're doing."

"Sometimes it seems like we must give and give and continue to give in order to win the game."

what the game teaches us about teamwork

The Broken Squares game is an experiential exercise that helps people create a shift in thinking about teamwork. The game simply acts as a catalyst to make them aware of their thought habits regarding teamwork, and how those thought habits lead to behaviors that either help or hinder their organization's results.

Game Barriers: When playing broken squares, people often notice the following behaviors that create barriers to playing the game effectively:

- **Protecting one's own square:** Trying to win individually
- **Checking out/quitting:** Allowing others to play for them; stopping once the individual objective is reached
- **Taking over:** Trying to play for others
- **Hoarding:** Keeping pieces rather than giving them away
- **Bending the rules:** Taking pieces, working on someone else's square
- **Judging:** Criticizing yourself and others
- **Refusing assistance:** Not allowing others to help

Workplace Barriers: Because you take your thinking with you wherever you go, the same behaviors that hindered your effectiveness in the Broken Squares game can create barriers for you at work. Some frequent barriers seen in the workplace are:

- **Criticizing others:** Other departments/other people, not understanding their objectives and problems, playing win-lose
- **Hoarding:** Resources and information
- **We/they:** Between different groups; competition vs. cooperation
- **Restricting the flow of information:** Everything from the top down; no upward flow; little cross-functional flow

Success Factors: Some behaviors and thinking or thought habits during the game contributed to success. Which of the following did you notice?

- **Trust:** Willingness to take risks
- **Looking at the big picture:** Looking beyond "my square" and "my table"
- **Willingness:** To give, as well as receive
- **Staying involved:** Even after the individual's square is complete
- **Commitment to the team objective:** The game is not over until all teams complete their squares
- **A bias for action:** Taking action vs. sitting back

senn delaney
the culture-shaping firm

HEIDRICK & STRUGGLES   © 1994-2017 Senn Delaney Leadership Consulting Group, LLC. All rights reserved.

CALVIN AND HOBBES; © 1994 Watterson Reprinted with permission of Universal Press Syndicate. All rights reserved

teamwork and the quality of thought

As we discussed in chapter one on (the "Human Operating System"), our behavior is driven by our thought habits and the quality of our thinking in any moment.

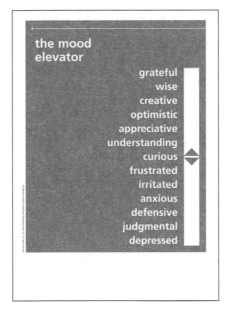

Look at the behaviors in the "Workplace Barriers" on the previous page. These behaviors are driven by lower-quality thoughts, and are accompanied by feelings on the lower end of the mood elevator, such as judgment, defensiveness, impatience or self-righteousness.

Now look at the list of behaviors under "Success Factors" on the previous page. These are all behaviors that are driven by higher-quality thinking, and are accompanied by feelings on the upper end of the mood elevator such as cooperation, curiosity, flexibility, creativity or patience.

When we are operating from high-quality thinking, the benefits of teamwork are obvious: what to do to be an effective team player is obvious; how to work together effectively with teammates is obvious. These behaviors come naturally. The key to being a high-performing team player is being aware of how you feel, or your mood. Using your moods and feelings as indicators of the quality of your thinking can help you to choose more effective behaviors, which will lead to better teamwork and better results for you, your team and your organization.

© 1994-2017 Senn Delaney Leadership Consulting Group, LLC All rights reserved

teamwork and trust

Bring to mind a relationship in your life where you have a strong feeling of trust. What is it about the relationship that creates that feeling of trust?

A major requirement for effective teamwork is trust. Accomplishing the group's objectives in an environment of mistrust is like trying to drive a car with the emergency brake on. In this type of environment people are distracted, fearful, angry, sensitive to slights, protective of turf and concerned only with their own goals. They are hesitant because they are concerned about how their actions may be judged or how failure might be perceived.

How do organizations build an environment of trust? Here are some tangible ways to increase the level of trust within a culture:

Respect: In collaborative cultures, people treat each other with respect.

- In meetings and discussions, people listen respectfully to everyone's ideas, without judgment, perhaps even encouraging diverse points of view and being open to seeing the merit in those ideas.

- People give one another credit where it's due; they use coaching and feedback to stay on track and to assist the development of team members.

- Leadership is shared, allowing everyone to step up to their own unique leadership capabilities.

Openness: Healthy cultures arise from an environment of openness. People feel free to say not only what they think, but also what they feel, no matter how silly or unreasonable it may sound. This requires an atmosphere of non-judgment, where people are not afraid to bring up agendas, conflicts or controversial issues.

Keep Agreements: In high-performing teams and cultures, people feel they can count on each other. This means that people need to keep their agreements with each other—they should do what they say they are going to do. And if it doesn't happen, people then need to feel permission to talk openly to each other about it.

Accountability: Success occurs when people feel individually accountable for the success of the entire team or organization. There is a feeling that everyone is in the same boat, all headed in the same direction, with the same overall intentions. Not only do people feel accountable for the success of the larger team, they also feel accountable for the success of each individual member.

summary

Today's organizations require teamwork and collaborative cultures to achieve their goals. While many people and organizations still hold to the ideal of the "heroic individual," teamwork actually allows us to achieve more, because a team is more than the sum of its parts. Teamwork optimizes the collective strengths of each of its members.

The Broken Squares game illustrates how every member of the organization contributes to its success. The behaviors that added to or detracted from the game's success are the same behaviors that likewise affect the success of the various teams on which we play in our work and personal lives. Being a good team player requires trust, respect, commitment, a big-picture viewpoint and a willingness to take action and to give and receive support.

senn delaney
the culture-shaping firm

HEIDRICK & STRUGGLES   © 1994-2017 Senn Delaney Leadership Consulting Group, LLC. All rights reserved.

Below is another example of how good teamwork can get people where they are going quicker and easier than they would on their own.

goose sense

Next fall when you see geese heading south for the winter flying along in a "V" formation, you might be interested in knowing what science has discovered about why they fly that way. As each bird flaps its wings, it creates an uplift for the bird immediately following. By flying in formation, the whole flock adds at least 71% greater flying range than if each bird flew on its own.

Whenever a goose falls out of formation, it suddenly feels the drag and resistance of trying to go it alone and quickly gets back into formation to take advantage of the lifting power of the bird immediately in front of it.

> If we have as much sense as a goose, we will stay in formation with those who are headed the same way we are going.

When the lead goose gets tired, he rotates back in the wing and another goose flies point.

> It pays to take turns doing hard jobs—with people or with geese flying south. These geese honk from behind to encourage those up front to keep up their speed. What do we say when we "honk from behind"?

Finally, when a goose gets sick or is wounded by gunshot and falls out, two geese fall out of formation and follow him down to help and protect him. They stay with him until he is either able to fly or until he is dead, and then they launch out on their own with another formation to catch up with their group.

> If we have the sense of a goose, we will stand by each other like that.[27]

© 1994-2017 Senn Delaney Leadership Consulting Group, LLC. All rights reserved.

questions, action steps and assignments

Creating an collaborative environment in your organization is well worth the effort. Use the following to help you determine what steps you need to take to develop better teamwork in your culture:

1. If you played the Broken Squares game, what assumptions did you make? What thought habits might have guided your actions? (Examples: The end justifies the means—win at all costs. If I accept or ask for assistance, it is a sign of weakness or incompetence.)

    _____

    _____

    _____

    _____

    _____

2. Using the learning from this chapter, assess the areas within your organization that you can influence. How could those areas benefit from better teamwork? What could you do to help make this happen?

    _____

    _____

    _____

    _____

    _____

3. Where are the breakdowns in teamwork? What is causing them? (i.e., lack of open communication, hidden agendas, lack of trust, lack of empowerment, lack of accountability, etc.) What can you do to address these breakdowns?

    _____

    _____

    _____

    _____

senn delaney
the culture-shaping firm

HEIDRICK & STRUGGLES

© 1994-2017 Senn Delaney Leadership Consulting Group, LLC. All rights reserved.

9

change

change: creating an agile culture

> "Whenever you face the steepening slope of change, that's when you need bold leadership. When premises are being challenged, that's when you need wise leadership."[28]
>
> Bernadine Healy, former director of the National Institutes of Health

With the ever-accelerating pace of today's business, organizational agility has become a vital cultural attribute, and the ability to manage change effectively a necessary leadership skill. Successfully leading change can be a tremendous challenge since resistance to change seems to be a natural human response to it. Many leaders underestimate the level of resistance they will encounter when attempting to implement something new. As a result, they also underestimate the time and resources needed for implementation.

In order to become even more effective leaders and change agents, we must learn to lead change differently by understanding and anticipating resistance, as well as to develop more effective strategies to introduce change and minimize the barriers it can create.

The first step is to develop a better respect and understanding of how and why people tend to react to change. Think back to the last major change you experienced in your life. As you do, consider these questions:

- How did you react when you heard about the change?
- How did the people around you react? Were the reactions uniform or mixed?
- Did you see the change as an opportunity or a threat?
- What feelings did you experience? Fear? Elation? Anxiety? Anticipation? Uncertainty? Confusion? Relief?
- What were some of the thoughts you had?
- Did you feel you had any control over the process? Or the way you thought or felt about it?
- Upon reflection, was there anything that happened to help you see the positive potential of that change?

© 1994-2017 Senn Delaney Leadership Consulting Group, LLC. All rights reserved.

HEIDRICK & STRUGGLES

why do people resist change?

Imagine for a moment that you have been working for the "Ajax Company" for seven years. You know your job well and get a lot of satisfaction from accomplishing your work efficiently. While you are not best friends with all of your co-workers, you've built up a good foundation of trust and respect and you enjoy being with them. As with any job, there are problems and occasional crises, but you have a high level of confidence in your ability to handle anything that comes up. You have received several promotions over the years and you believe your manager tries to treat everyone fairly.

One day your leader calls your group together and announces that the company has been purchased and is being reorganized. She says that's all she knows so there isn't any point in trying to answer any questions right now, and she will let you know as soon as she knows more.

Suddenly your future isn't as clear. You don't know if your job will change, or even whether there will ultimately be a job available for you in the new organization.

How do you think you might react?

How do you think you would feel?

Drawing by R. Morgan; ©1994, SDLCG

change perspective

The results of a University of California Medical Center study on organizations going through significant change may give us some insight into how people would typically respond to such a change. The study found that 20% of employees going through a change actually embrace the change and herald it as a great event. Another 20% have a negative reaction to the change. The remaining 60% have varying levels of resistance to the change. The reactions to change varied significantly although the tangible impact of the change was similar for all employees in the study.

HEIDRICK & STRUGGLES   © 1994-2017 Senn Delaney Leadership Consulting Group, LLC. All rights reserved.

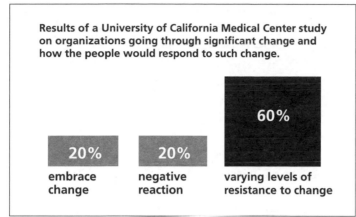

Results of a University of California Medical Center study on organizations going through significant change and how the people would respond to such change.

60%

20% — embrace change

20% — negative reaction

varying levels of resistance to change

The study concluded that the primary reason for the difference in level of resistance was the employee's attitude or perspective.[29] In other words, the employees' response to the change came not from the event itself, but from their thinking about the event.

The same is true for every change we face, regardless of circumstance. Have you ever been frightened or frustrated about a change and after a good night's sleep, realized that everything looked different? Your circumstance didn't change; you merely saw things differently because the quality of your thinking shifted.

When faced with the unknown, our imaginations can become very active. We often try to make a connection to a similar past event, and based on the outcome of that event, we project how this one will affect us in the future. Often we imagine the worst. Those thoughts frame our perspective to the change, and the resulting feelings are the basis for our reaction.

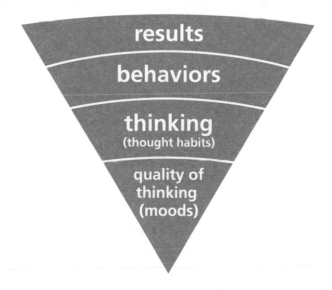

results

behaviors

thinking
(thought habits)

quality of thinking
(moods)

creating a healthy change attitude

In the study mentioned on the previous page, the researchers also found three attitude influencers that were especially important to how an employee fared in the environment of change.

senn delaney
the culture-shaping firm

HEIDRICK & STRUGGLES

© 1994-2017 Senn Delaney Leadership Consulting Group, LLC. All rights reserved.

- **Hopeful Perspective:** Employees who as a rule didn't resist the change, but viewed it as an opportunity and a challenge, fared better emotionally and physically. Those who saw it as an opportunity put their energies into participating in the change rather than resisting it.

- **Perceived Control:** Those employees who still felt they could contribute and make a difference, even in the face of change, remained more positive and fared well. Those who felt victimized did not tend to do as well emotionally or physically.

- **Level of Commitment:** Employees with a high level of commitment to their job, the company, and the overall mission tolerated the change much better than people who did not feel committed and thus felt the change was just a way of manipulating them.[30]

Since the world is constantly changing, we don't have much choice about whether or not we will face change. Considering the above, perhaps the more important question is, how can we become even more effective when faced with change?

One way is to become more aware that your thinking creates your feelings and reactions. Remember what the Mood Elevator tells us about the quality of our thinking: fear, insecurity, frustration, impatience, defensiveness and judgment are feelings we have when we are experiencing lower-quality thinking. When have these feelings, we have a natural tendency to resist the proposed change and an urge to return to the way things were.

The amount of perspective we have will come from our awareness of how we feel. This, in turn, will determine how effective we are as leaders and team members in leading, responding to and positively influencing others.

creating a "change-oriented" culture

Thriving in today's world of change requires a culture that doesn't wait for change, but rather one that seeks it out and encourages innovation. There are three major steps to creating a culture that encourages innovation:

- Develop "possibility thinking"
- Train and encourage participant/supporter/coach behaviors
- Understand the steps in effective implementation of change

Possibility Thinking

One way to understand whether (or not) an organization has a healthy perspective toward change is to observe how it responds to new ideas. Creating an environment where people feel free to generate and share new ideas and to innovate is critical to thriving in today's rapidly changing business environment. Moreover, the freedom to try out new ideas requires a culture that does not punish the mistakes and failures that naturally accompany new ventures.

Remarkably, few organizations actively encourage the sharing of ideas, especially if they are considered outside the "normal" boundaries.

senn delaney
the culture-shaping firm

HEIDRICK & STRUGGLES © 1994-2017 Senn Delaney Leadership Consulting Group, LLC. All rights reserved.

When presented with an idea for a new type of wheelbarrow like the one pictured above, most of us would tend to focus on the reasons why it wouldn't work:

> "The handle is too short."

> "The hopper is too deep."

> "It's a stupid design."

> "It's out of balance."

> "It would be impossible to empty."

Many of us have developed the habit of focusing on the obstacles. This habit can sometimes help us to identify problems, prevent mistakes and avoid errors.

The hazard of relying on this habit is that when we respond to a new idea by focusing on the obstacles, we kill our employee's impulse to generate more new ideas. Worse yet, we send the message to others: "Don't share ideas here!"

If we want to encourage the generation of ideas, we need a different mindset. When children see the wheelbarrow illustration, they give us an entirely different set of responses:

> "That's interesting—the handle is so short, if you got mud on the wheel you could just kick it off."

> "It would be easy to empty it in a hole because you could wheel it right up to the edge. What if you had a little trap door at the bottom that you could open with a string?"

It could be that they just are not as familiar with what a wheelbarrow should look like. As adults, our preconceived notions of what a solution should look like often prevent us from seeing and finding truly innovative, effective solutions. Children, however, seem to naturally exude possibility thinking.

Possibility thinking doesn't mean ignoring what's wrong with an idea, it means looking beyond the flaws to see if an idea has possibilities. We look for the "golden nuggets" buried beneath the obvious. This is critical because almost all new ideas are a mixture of positives and negatives, and many of them look strange at first. However, if we throw out an idea as soon as we see a negative, we will be throwing out lots of possibilities that might contain even bigger positives.

© 1994-2017 Senn Delaney Leadership Consulting Group, LLC. All rights reserved.

By permission of Leigh Rubin and Creators Syndicate, Inc.

Not surprisingly, possibility thinking is a characteristic of high-quality thinking. We know when we are open to possibility thinking by paying attention to our feelings and moods. Just as our response to change is directly determined by our moods, so is our ability to share and appreciate new ideas. When we're on the upper end of the Mood Elevator, we experience higher-quality thinking, or possibility thinking. In that state, we are able to see both sides: the positive and the negative. It allows us to look at new ideas and see the possibilities as well as the defects.

Organizations that want to encourage innovation need to foster a flexible culture that welcomes new ideas. In such a culture, employees feel free to offer ideas, even when they are not perfectly crafted, without fear of criticism or punishment. They are allowed the freedom to occasionally make mistakes in pursuit of achieving excellence. This type of culture creates more choices, and since it encourages innovation and growth, it achieves better results.

Participant/Supporter/Coach Behaviors

One way to evaluate your performance as a leader relative to encouraging positive change is to ask yourself how often people come to you with their new ideas.

Next, consider whether your behavior towards new ideas is more likely to be critical or encouraging. Critics tend to find the flaws in ideas while coaches encourage people to share their ideas and to make them better.

Here are typical behaviors of each:

Critic (observer/critic/judge)	Coach (participant/supporter/coach)
Focuses on defects and problems	Focuses on desired results
Identifies barriers	Finds ways to make it work
Shoots holes in ideas	Finds golden nuggets in ideas
Listens in order to judge or criticize	Listens in order to understand and discuss
Interrupts, nitpicks	Allows time for full discussion
Judges the presenter harshly; uses put-downs	Is considerate of others and their points of view
Punishes wild ideas and failures	Encourages new ideas and risk taking

HEIDRICK & STRUGGLES   © 1994-2017 Senn Delaney Leadership Consulting Group, LLC. All rights reserved.

Most corporate cultures have historically emphasized the skills of the critic rather than the coach. Many leaders have operated under the philosophy that it is better to keep doing things the way they've always been done rather than risk a mistake by doing something different. Managers were taught to look for and solve problems, which emphasized their skills as a critic. In fact, many managers pride themselves on being a "devil's advocate": one who challenges ideas, and actively looks for reasons why they won't work.

Drawing by R. Morgan; ©1994, SDLCG

Being the recipient of such an approach and having to defend new ideas constantly requires a great deal of extra effort and energy. Imagine how much more productive people would be if they could use that energy elsewhere: perhaps generating even more creative ideas!

The behavior of critics is typically the result of thought habits that they've developed over the years. In a lower mood, these thoughts seem very real, and it's difficult to break out of them, or even to be aware that they are affecting us. Being aware of our moods and the choices we have will enable us to spend more time in the more effective position, the coach.

Here are other ways you can help people in your organization learn new participant/supporter/coach skills:

- **Be a role model** and try to look for the possibilities in ideas. Suspend your judgment, particularly if you catch yourself in a low mood, and look beyond the obvious.

- **Give others constructive feedback** when you see them displaying critical behaviors, and encouragement when they are acting as a coach.

- **Set up ground rules** for meetings and brainstorming sessions. Pay attention to the overall mood of the meeting. Establish guidelines to delay judgment and evaluation until after the idea generation portion has ended.

- **Have group discussions** about what types of behaviors are most effective for stimulating new ideas.

- **Put signs or other reminders** on walls, desks, etc., To remind people to be open to new ideas, possibility thinking and to be a coach versus a critic.

© 1994-2017 Senn Delaney Leadership Consulting Group, LLC. All rights reserved.

HEIDRICK & STRUGGLES

"... and I want you to find the wise guy who rotated my sign."

Dave Blazek © 2004, Tribune Media Services. Reprinted with permission.

effective implementation of change

Once the need for change has been determined, there are several steps that will reduce resistance and aid in implementation. Remember, we can only influence others to the extent that we are "walking the talk." Actions speak louder than words.

Prior to introducing any change, walk through the following steps:

- **Be aware of how you feel:** First check your mood elevator. What's the quality of your thinking like? If it's low, try and wait until you have more perspective before talking to others about the impending change (unless you're seeking coaching from someone who will help you get perspective). Secondly, be understanding. While you have the liberty of checking your mood prior to talking to others about change, we can never be sure everyone is experiencing higher-quality thinking. Know that others experiencing the change are doing the best they can given their thinking. Resistance, discomfort and insecurity can be natural responses. Try not to be judgmental; people can and will usually get past their initial reactions. Know that while you can be a positive influence, it's important to give people time to process things in their own way. The more you can maintain perspective during times of change, the more supportive you can be of others.

- **Communicate the why:** Even though at times it seems like an extra step, helping people understand why a change makes sense or is necessary can save a lot of time and effort in the long run. To help others understand and accept the change, begin by sharing from your perspective why the change makes sense to you, not just what the change is. It's also important to understand that everyone sees the world differently, so encourage others to share their understanding in a healthy way. It is critical that people develop their own understanding of why a change makes sense to them.

- **Exhibit vision and commitment to the change:** To be successful, a change effort needs a driving force leading the charge—a champion who has an unflappable belief in the value of the change.

- **Listen to what people say:** People want to be heard and feel that they can air their concerns, questions and complaints without fear of judgment or retribution. Typically, once people feel that they are being heard, they are much more willing to let go of any

HEIDRICK & STRUGGLES   © 1994-2017 Senn Delaney Leadership Consulting Group, LLC. All rights reserved.

resistance they might be holding onto. This is a real opportunity for leaders to Be Here Now. Open discussions of the change can also reveal valid frustrations that, if addressed, may make the change effort more successful.

- **Get people involved:** Encourage them to express their ideas and feelings about the change. Ask for ideas about implementing the change. Try to get as many people as possible involved in designing the implementation plan. When people feel involved in the process of change, they are more likely to be emotionally invested in it and will work toward making it a success. Getting people involved also gives them a sense of control over the outcome, which relieves some of the stress involved with change.

- **Communicate…communicate…communicate:** If anything, err on the side of over-communicating during times of change. Give people lots of information about the change. Make it easy for them to know how they will be affected and what the overall plan is. Give them opportunities to ask questions and voice opinions. Even if there are things you can't tell them, at least openly acknowledge that fact, perhaps explaining why you can't tell them those things. Often resistance to change is a result of fear of the unknown. People may assume the worst as their imaginations fill in the gaps in their knowledge.

- **Weed out the hard-core resisters:** Some people will not be able to adapt to the new environment. While they should be given a reasonable chance to become a part of the change, if it appears that they cannot or will not support the new direction, they need to be reassigned or let go. This should be done with care and compassion, but it must be done or the entire change process will be sabotaged, not only by the person who refuses to support the change, but by others who see that person remaining in place.

- **Create early success:** Success breeds success, so try to structure the change process so that early efforts bring visible successful results. This should include celebrating these early successes and reinforcing all behaviors aligned with the change. Frequent feedback and coaching needs to be a regular part of the implementation plan.

Leaders who want to be successful change agents require many skills. Todd D. Jick said it well in "Managing Change":

> "…the change agent needs the sensitivity of a social worker, the insights of a psychologist, the stamina of a marathon runner, the persistence of a bulldog, the self-reliance of a hermit, and the patience of a saint. And even with all those qualities, there is no guarantee of success."[31]

While there may be no guarantee of success, the leaders who understand their own reactions to change and anticipate their group's resistance to proposed changes can develop an implementation plan that is much more likely to succeed.

emotional cycle of change

Even though as a leader you understand the foundation of resistance and follow through by doing everything possible to reduce the resistance, you can still be lulled into a false sense of security by the emotional cycle of change:

© 1994-2017 Senn Delaney Leadership Consulting Group, LLC. All rights reserved.

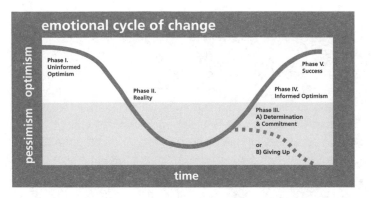

Phase I—Honeymoon: Once a change is underway and people begin to see the possible payoffs, there is a "honeymoon" period. People get excited and energized by the possibilities.

Phase II—Discouragement: At some point, reality hits and people begin to realize that it is an uphill battle. People can get discouraged and uncertain about whether they can succeed.

Phase III—Renewal: This is the critical phase. Either commitment to the change is renewed and people proceed with a better understanding of the effort needed to succeed, or they give up. Many change projects never make it past this point.

Phase IV—Informed Optimism: People are determined to reach their goals and they know what obstacles they have to overcome to get there.

Phase V—Success: People are elated because they have accomplished their objective. They need to celebrate and be honored for their efforts.

Paying strict attention to the section on effective implementation of change will help minimize the negative effects of this cycle, particularly in Phase III.

a "blessing in disguise?"

We've all had the experience of being faced with a change, not wanting to do it, resisting it wholeheartedly, and then afterwards being happy about it—feeling it was a blessing in disguise.

Think of an example like that in your life. What was the "blessing in disguise?"

Remember that people around you will go through the same feelings you did, so bring that understanding to the table. And also remember that they will land on their feet and may even end up thanking you.

Calvin and Hobbes, ©1993, Watterson. Reprinted with permission of Universal Press Syndicate. All rights reserved.

HEIDRICK & STRUGGLES   © 1994-2017 Senn Delaney Leadership Consulting Group, LLC. All rights reserved.

summary

Change is inevitable, and quite often beyond our control. However, the key determinant to how well we handle change is very much within our control: our attitude.

To foster a healthy change attitude in yourself and others, remember:

- Develop "possibility thinking" toward new ideas and different ways of getting results.
- Exhibit and encourage participant/supporter/coach behaviors: take time to listen and discuss; focus on desired results rather than problems and obstacles; coach vs. criticize.
- Understand the effects and implications of change, and take some time to create and execute an effective implementation plan.

© 1994-2017 Senn Delaney Leadership Consulting Group, LLC. All rights reserved.

senn delaney
the culture-shaping firm

HEIDRICK & STRUGGLES

questions, action steps and assignments

Take a moment and think of a time when you were encouraged to be innovative and suggest new ideas. What was that environment like? If you have never worked in that type of environment, try to imagine it.

1. What can leaders do to foster more "possibility thinking" in their teams?

_____

_____

_____

_____

_____

_____

2. What are your strengths in implementing change as a change agent?

_____

_____

_____

_____

_____

_____

3. What could you do to be more of a coach and encourage more innovative ideas within your team?

_____

_____

_____

_____

_____

_____

4. Think about a specific change that you would like to implement. What could you do to ensure its successful implementation?

_____

_____

_____

_____

© 1994-2017 Senn Delaney Leadership Consulting Group, LLC. All rights reserved.

10

coaching and feedback

High-performance cultures are those where people live the essential values like accountability and teamwork. So how do we increase the probability that people will exhibit these values and behaviors? What motivates people to act accountably, to grow and learn and to do their best?

Reflect on what motivates you to do your best.

For years, the theory of motivation revolved around the carrot and the stick. Managers were taught that motivating people was a matter of rewarding them for good actions and punishing them for bad actions. We now know that human motivation is much more complex than that. While people respond to a variety of motivating factors, we have found the common denominator is that most people want to have feedback on how they are doing, and they want it in a constructive and positive manner. They want to know they are making a difference, and that it is recognized.

appreciative and constructive feedback

Appreciative feedback is probably the simplest and least expensive method of motivating and rewarding people. It's also the first step in the coaching process. Saying thanks, sending personal notes, posting complimentary letters from customers and celebrating outstanding efforts are simple, inexpensive ways to let people know you appreciate and value them.

In addition, it is useful for people to know specifically what they are doing well. As illustrated in the blindfolded dart throw exercise you experienced in the unfreezing session, employees need to know which behaviors cause them to hit the target or get close to it. This is **appreciative** feedback, and it is just as valuable as feedback on the behaviors that cause us to miss the target.

Imagine for a moment teaching an infant how to walk. How successful would the infant be if we focused on the falls or mistakes instead of enthusiastically applauding their efforts? With infants, we catch them doing something approximately right and then appreciate them for it. This increases the probability that they will try it again, or repeat the behavior. The same principle applies with grown-ups. Feedback that is always **constructive** and never **appreciative** eventually becomes discouraging and unproductive.

© 1994-2017 Senn Delaney Leadership Consulting Group, LLC. All rights reserved.

On the other side of the equation, if people only receive appreciative feedback, they will never know how to improve. If the appreciative feedback seems sugary or always warm and fuzzy, it can seem shallow and superficial, affecting neither performance nor the person's sense of appreciation.

So it is just as vital to provide **constructive** feedback on how to improve performance. Most every-one wants to know how to be more effective. Studies done by Lawrence J. Bradford and Claire Raines and published in their book *Twentysomething* show that most employees do not feel they receive enough appreciative or constructive feedback. If people do not know how they are doing, they do not know what to change to do better.[32]

A healthy, growth-oriented work environment is one that is **feedback-rich**. It provides the information people need to continuously improve their performance.

criticism versus constructive feedback

Many people assume that constructive feedback is the same as criticism. Although the terms are often used interchangeably, there is a vast difference in how the two are received. Even the roots of the words differ greatly. Critic means to judge value, while construct means to build up. Here are some other implied differences between the two:

Criticism	Constructive Feedback
Past orientation	Future orientation
Personal focus	Behavior focus
Negative tone	Positive tone
Problem-oriented	Solution-oriented

Criticism generally comes in "here's what you did wrong" words while constructive feedback comes in "here's how you can do better next time" words.

Peanuts: © United Feature Syndicate, Inc.

HEIDRICK & STRUGGLES   © 1994-2017 Senn Delaney Leadership Consulting Group, LLC. All rights reserved.

coaching versus venting

Coaching and giving feedback are avenues of assisting people to reach their full potential. Sometimes, however, coaching can be confused with venting, or letting someone know when you're bothered, irritated or even angry about something the other person has done or said.

Have you ever become upset with someone because you thought they had deliberately done something to you, only to find that it was an innocent and unintended action? For example, when a person with an analytical style asks for a lot of data from a promoting style who dislikes data, their intention is not to irritate. They are just doing what comes naturally to them.

Coaching should not be used as an excuse for "getting something off your chest." In that mode, the last thing on your mind is the other person's overall success and development. A good guideline to follow in terms of timing is: If you feel compelled to give feedback, it is probably not the right time.

Tips for giving feedback:

- Spend some time preparing a clear, succinct message to clarify expectations—don't give constructive feedback on the spur of the moment.
- Be clear on the direction and purpose of coaching/feedback.
- Be Here Now.
- Avoid "locking in" to a specific outcome; be willing to listen to the other person's viewpoint.
- Use "I" statements to emphasize that the feedback is opinion, rather than fact.
- Talk about behavior, not the person.
- Help the person to see specific application.
- Talk optimistically about the future, rather than disparagingly about the past.
- Make sure your own behavior is consistent with your message.

beliefs that can limit coaching

Most managers and leaders have good intentions, but the daily demands of work life often distract them from providing feedback even though they know they should. Think about your personal situation. Do you give your employees or teammates enough feedback? If you answered no, think about some of the reasons you don't.

© 1994-2017 Senn Delaney Leadership Consulting Group, LLC All rights reserved.

senn delaney
the culture-shaping firm

HEIDRICK & STRUGGLES

The results cone above graphically depicts how our thinking creates our behaviors and ultimately our results. Below is a list of the often-unconscious thought habits or beliefs that can prevent coaching. As you read them, think about which ones might be limiting your ability to coach effectively.

Examples of Thought Habits/Limiting Beliefs

For Appreciative Feedback:

- It might sound insincere.

- They might get embarrassed.

- It is more important to tell them what is wrong so they can improve.

- They might ask for a raise.

- They might start to slack off.

- It is their job to do well.

- People know when they are doing well; I should not have to tell them.

In the session, people are given the opportunity to both give and receive appreciative feedback. Many people are very moved by that experience and have an insight that appreciative feedback helps people to be at their best. They find that giving appreciative feedback becomes much easier and more natural and begin doing it more often, which results in better performance all around.

For Constructive Feedback:

- They might get mad.

- I might not say it right.

- They are professionals; they should know what they need to do.

- It is not my job.

- It takes too much time.

- I might be misunderstood.

- I do not know enough of the details, so I should not say anything.

The blindfolded dart throw exercise often leads to insights that neglecting to offer useful feedback or guidance is not just a missed opportunity to help others, but is, in a way, letting people down. As these habitual beliefs begin to make less sense, it becomes much easier to approach people with useful, constructive feedback and supportive coaching.

Experiencing insight helps people to see thought habits for what they are, and causes the thought habits to quickly begin to lose their power.

the consequences of not coaching

Whatever the beliefs about one's own personal coaching abilities, it cannot be denied that the lack of coaching carries with it some very undesirable byproducts. One of these is the presence of hidden agendas within an organization. **Hidden agendas** are created when people do not communicate openly or provide appropriate feedback to each other. Hidden agendas are unspoken messages between people, marked by often-inaccurate assumptions of ulterior motives. As hidden agendas

HEIDRICK & STRUGGLES   © 1994-2017 Senn Delaney Leadership Consulting Group, LLC. All rights reserved.

increase, resentment and tension build, further blocking communication and trust. Arguments, labor disputes, divorce and even war are often the result of a long build-up of hidden agendas.

Communication deteriorates rapidly when hidden agendas are complicated by communication triangles. This happens in the following way:

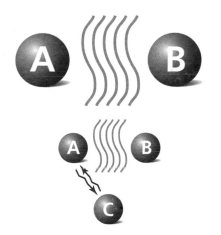

A is unhappy with **B** but does not say anything to **B**

A goes to **C** and talks about the awful thing B did

B is now further alienated from **A**, and **C** feels caught in the middle

Whatever **A** was unhappy about has almost no chance of getting fixed. Have you ever been in an environment where it seemed that everyone knew what you were doing wrong except you? What does that do to productivity? ...to trust?

BEETLE BAILEY: © Reprinted with special permission of King Features Syndicate.

an historical view of coaching

The traditional coaching model assumes a hierarchical relationship between a student and an expert. This model places a tremendous burden on each role. The student will eventually come to rely on the coach for all guidance and direction and feel less and less empowered to make the appropriate choices himself or to generalize the learning to broader contexts. The burden for the coach is the need to have the answers. Needing to respond to a multitude of problems, the traditional coach relies upon a system of steps, tools, and techniques. The downside is that the advice can be stale, losing its relevance to the student's underlying need for growth, and often cannot be replicated.

© 1994-2017 Senn Delaney Leadership Consulting Group, LLC. All rights reserved.

senn delaney
the culture-shaping firm

HEIDRICK & STRUGGLES

"Norman, please—just tell us, are we doing good, or are we doing bad?"
©1993 by Sidney Harris—Harvard Business Review.

what is a good coach

Most of us can look back on our lives and recognize at least one person who was an excellent coach for us: a team sports coach, teacher, parent, relative, friend, supervisor or religious advisor. This person cared enough to help us develop our skills and capabilities.

Think about the people who have coached you during your life. What value did they give you through their coaching (helped you with a specific skill, gave you self-confidence, helped you reach a goal, introduced you to a new idea or way of thinking, etc.)? Did the value come from the content of what they told you, or from the relationship you had with them? Did your coach give you all the answers, or give you the means to realize solutions on your own?

the rapport-based view of coaching

While the traditional approach to coaching uses an "outside-in" approach to change behavior, rapport coaching is more of an "inside-out" approach, which leads to the creation of insights on the part of the person being coached. This model is built on the premise that through effective coaching, employees can personally learn and discover relevant solutions to the challenges they encounter.

Instead of advising the employee to perform a series of behavioral tasks, the rapport coach focuses on each person's innate ability to access their own creative answers. In this case, the coach's role is not only to point out where the employee is failing to perform or negatively affecting others through their behavior, but also to guide the employee to become more aware of the thinking and state of mind behind their behavior. This process removes the burden and limitations of the coach to provide problem-specific answers and leads the employee to insights about how to shift their behavior to be more effective and productive.

With this approach, coaching becomes more of a dynamic process that takes place in a climate of partnership and discovery. The advantage of uncovering the source of personal and organizational creativity is that the learning is generalized to any situation that might be encountered. The rapport

HEIDRICK & STRUGGLES   © 1994-2017 Senn Delaney Leadership Consulting Group, LLC. All rights reserved.

coach makes no assumption as to why behaviors occur, and understands that if people knew an easier or more effective way to do things, they would naturally behave differently. A personal transformation occurs with the understanding that the source of this power is internal rather than external.

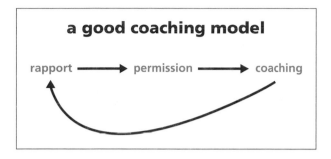

The next section lists the collective elements that make up the rapport coaching model. While these elements are listed in a sequential order, they do not occur in a linear fashion. The coach is constantly moving back and forth among the elements to ensure the coaching session is on track.

a good coaching model: rapport>permission>coach

Effective coaching requires establishing rapport. No matter how constructive your feedback is, if the person is not receptive to hearing it, it cannot be effective. Most people describe rapport as having a connection with another person: a sense of relaxation, trust and support.

The first step in gaining rapport is to check the Mood Elevator. How are you feeling? What is the quality of your thinking? On the Mood Elevator diagram below, where do you think you would be most effective in terms of giving and receiving feedback?

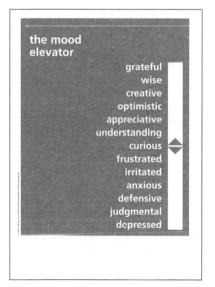

Another way to make sure you are in rapport is to pay attention to how you are listening. We all operate at different levels of listening at different times. As a coach, just understanding the different levels will make you aware of your own tendencies. This will help you shift, as required, to the most appropriate level of listening throughout your coaching dialogue. There is more information on listening on the following page.

© 1994-2017 Senn Delaney Leadership Consulting Group, LLC. All rights reserved.

HEIDRICK & STRUGGLES

Remember that your goal is to create the best environment possible to ensure that the person thinks about your feedback. Asking **permission** demonstrates respect for their state of mind and their readiness to receive feedback. Without readiness and receptivity, the message will be ignored or resented. Remember also that asking for permission implies a willingness to accept that the person may not be ready to hear you.

Once you have rapport and permission, the **coaching** dialogue can begin.

Throughout the coaching dialogue, listening with openness and lack of limiting preconceptions allows the coach to have the perspective to see beyond the surface content and to appreciate the thinking that generates the other person's behavior. In this way, finding solutions will be a mutual process that is intuitive and rewarding.

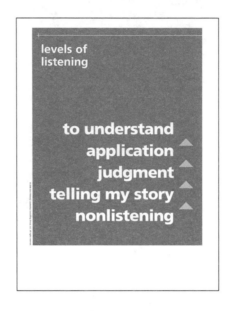

In the chapter titled "Be Here Now," we introduced the concept of Levels of Listening. Deep listening, or listening to understand, is especially important when it comes to coaching others. The coach listens without distractions and is not provoked into judgment, application, or implication. The coach is open to the possibility of changing his/her viewpoint or seeing something not yet realized. Even if the coach does not agree, s/he can understand how a person could have the view being expressed. Empathy and compassion are hallmarks of listening for understanding, along with the ability to read between the lines.

The coach is not listening for any pre-conceived desired outcomes. This enables the coach to see things in a different light. This deeper listening allows the coach to then guide the other person towards insight and the ability to find their own solution.

HEIDRICK & STRUGGLES   © 1994-2017 Senn Delaney Leadership Consulting Group, LLC. All rights reserved.

summary

Coaching is also one of the most valuable things you can do for another person. A caring coach is a person who helps us reach our goals and achieve our full potential. In today's business world, which demands a continuous level of improvement, it is incumbent on today's leaders to help their people achieve excellence. From a strictly commercial standpoint, coaching is an essential leadership skill.

Rapport coaching involves three basic steps: Rapport, Permission, Coach.

Since rapport coaching is based upon exploring the thinking underlying the behavior, the effective coach ensures that rapport and permission are present, establishes a coaching dialogue and listens for understanding. By listening at this deeper level, coaches can help people connect to the underlying thinking that shapes their behaviors and gain the insights necessary to shift them.

© 1994-2017 Senn Delaney Leadership Consulting Group, LLC. All rights reserved.

HEIDRICK & STRUGGLES

questions, action steps and assignments

1. What are the key principles of effective coaching that make the most sense for you?

_____

_____

_____

_____

_____

2. What are your strengths as a coach? How could you be even more effective?

_____

_____

_____

_____

3. What level of listening tends to be your "default setting"? What are some ways you can begin to listen more effectively?

_____

_____

_____

_____

_____

4. Jot down the names of some people from whom you would like to receive more honest feedback. Next to their names, commit to a date by which you will have talked to them about your desire, and set up a coaching meeting.

_____

_____

_____

_____

5. In order to have the people in your area become coaches, you must role-model this activity yourself. Set up coaching meetings with each member of your staff. (Remember to listen!) After these sessions are held, request that all of them, in turn, do the same with their direct reports.

_____

_____

_____

_____

senn delaney
the culture-shaping firm

11

shadow of the leader

Actions speak louder than words.

Be a role model.

Set a good example.

Walk the talk.

Practice what you preach.

These familiar phrases have a common message: What we do is just as important, perhaps even more so, as what we say. The most effective leaders shape the culture of their organizations through a powerful combination of both behaviors and messages. Through our behaviors and messages, we cast a powerful shadow that influences everyone around us: in the workplace, at home and in the community.

The shadow that great leaders cast extends far beyond their own lives. Mother Teresa devoted her life to serving the impoverished, the orphaned, the disabled and the dying. The order she founded in Calcutta, Missionaries of Charity, now operates 700 missions serving the "poorest of the poor" in 183 countries. Even after her death in 1997, her example continues to inspire people around the world. After Nelson Mandela was imprisoned for his opposition to apartheid in South Africa, he went on to become the first black president of that country. Because of his moral integrity and per-severance to his ideals, he is a worldwide symbol of courage and resistance to racism.

But the concept of the shadow of the leader is not limited to world leaders. Each of us casts our own shadow, and in doing so we influence those around us. Consider the business leaders, teach-ers, parents, friends, peers, coaches, church and community leaders that have been influential in your life. How have their shadows influenced you? More than likely the strongest shadows were cast by those whose actions reinforced their words.

"A leader doesn't just get the message across—a leader is the message."[33]

Warren Bennis

© 1994-2017 Senn Delaney Leadership Consulting Group, LLC. All rights reserved.

the shadow at home

James Baldwin, the American author noted for his works on personal identity and civil rights, states, "Children have never been very good at listening to their elders, but they have never failed to imitate them." Any message can be drowned out by conflicting actions.

If you ask people what the first important influence in their lives was or where it came from, the majority will point to their parents. As a rule, home is where we first experience the shadow concept. Most parents learn quickly that encouraging their children to "Do as I say, not as I do," just doesn't work! Children generally tune out the words and mimic the behaviors they see because children are expert mimics. If you watch them at play, you can hear and see them mimic the adult behaviors that they've observed. "Like mother, like daughter" and "like father, like son" are more than just expressions.

These lines from Dorothy Law Nolte are a powerful reminder of our influence:

Children Learn What They Live

If children live with criticism, they learn to condemn.

If children live with hostility, they learn to fight.

If children live with ridicule, they learn to be shy.

If children live with shame, they learn to feel guilty.

If children live with tolerance, they learn to be patient.

If children live with encouragement, they learn confidence.

If children live with praise, they learn to appreciate.

If children live with fairness, they learn justice.

If children live with security, they learn to have faith.

If children live with approval, they learn to like themselves.

If children live with acceptance and friendship, they learn
   to find love in the world.[34]

The role of the leader, at work and at home, requires modeling the desired behavior and letting others see the desired values in action. Henry Wheeler Shaw once said: "To bring up a child in the way he should go, travel that way yourself once in a while." To become effective leaders, we must become aware of our shadow and then learn to make our actions match our message.

HEIDRICK & STRUGGLES   © 1994-2017 Senn Delaney Leadership Consulting Group, LLC. All rights reserved.

CATHY © 1994 Cathy Guisewite. Reprinted with permission of UNIVERSAL PRESS SYNDICATE. All Rights Reserved.

Think for a moment of characteristics you possess, beliefs you hold or habits you have that are also true of one or both of your parents:

My Mother/Father:

_____

_____

I also:

_____

_____

The following story illustrates how unconscious we can be about our behavior when it comes to our shadow:

> "One Sunday I noticed my wife cutting off the ends of a ham before baking it. When I asked her why she did it, she said, 'Oh, I don't know. That's just the way my mother always did it.'

> "The next time we were at her mother's, I asked her about it. She, too, said that was just the way her mother did it. Her mother happened to be in the next room, so I asked her about it. She said that when she was first married, their oven was too small for a whole ham, so she got in the habit of cutting off the ends before she baked it and she just never changed."

It's one thing to consciously influence others through coaching and teaching, but it's another to realize that we influence others by who we are and how we behave, without even trying!

"It's tough to keep up a messy room when your dad is a quality-control manager."

Drawing by Solinger; ©1993 The Saturday Evening Post

the shadow in the workplace

Good leaders know the importance of consistency between actions and words. Shelley A. Kirkpatrick and Edwin A. Locke addressed this issue in an article entitled, "Leadership: Do Traits Matter?"

> "Leaders must behave the way they wish their followers would behave. For example, if they want direct reports to be customer-oriented, they should spend time themselves talking to customers. This has far more influence on employees than just telling them that customers are important."[35]

One former insurance industry CEO phrased it in slightly stronger terms:

> "I would submit to you that it is unnatural for you to come in late and for your people to come in early. I think it is unnatural for you to be dishonest and your people to be honest...I think it is unnatural for you to not handle your finances well and then to expect your people to handle theirs well. In all these simple things, I think you have to set the standard."[36]

The shadow concept is very powerful within the business world. Think of a manager you worked for that you respected. What are some of the characteristics of that person that you acquired?

the shadow and group culture

The leader of a group casts a shadow that influences the group culture. Regardless of whether the shadow is weak or powerful, it always exists. It is a reflection of everything the leader does and says. Marjorie M. Blanchard, president of Blanchard Training and Development, Inc., describes it this way:

> "People are smart. If you say one thing and do another, people see the discrepancies. Every decision I make as a leader in my company is being watched for meaning and the values behind it. When you make a mistake, you create a negative story that can last a long time. So leaders have to lead by example, and be aware of the impact they create."[37]

Whole organizations often take on aspects of the personality of a strong leader. In 1948, then-chairman of the board William McKnight established a management philosophy at 3M that encouraged employee initiative, delegation of authority and a tolerance for mistakes in the pursuit of innovation. These remain 3M's guiding principles today. Microsoft is known for being innovative and competitive, a direct reflection of its founder and chairman Bill Gates.

senn delaney
the culture-shaping firm

HEIDRICK & STRUGGLES

© 1994-2017 Senn Delaney Leadership Consulting Group, LLC. All rights reserved.

Sometimes corporate cultures are so closely connected to the leader of the organization that it is almost impossible to think of the organization without thinking of the leader as well: for example, Gary Kelly at Southwest Airlines, Fred Smith at Federal Express, and Michael Dell at Dell Computers. This is the power of the shadow in action—the power to shape and influence the character of the organization.

how the shadow concept works: awareness is key

One of the primary motivators that causes people to mimic the shadow of others is the desire to have the respect and approval of people we consider to be important in our lives. This concept is seen in the workplace as employees work to gain the respect and approval of their manager or leader.

Most leaders have a difficult time understanding how to apply this concept simply because they are unaware of their own shadow. In addition, they are often unconscious of the behaviors, beliefs and attitudes they project. Many leaders do not fully realize the influence their behavior can have on an entire organization and, because of this, may be addressing the wrong issues in order to fix a particular problem.

The following is an example of how one leader influenced a trend without necessarily intending to:

> During a series of interviews with senior executives, a consultant noticed that most people used special stand-up workstations as they did their work. As he reviewed the results of his interviews with the CEO, who had joined the firm a short time before, he commented on how dynamic the executives were and how unusual it was to see everyone using the stand-up desks in their offices. The president chuckled and said, "Isn't it funny to see? I've been wondering why there have been so many requisitions for these since I came here. The only reason I use one is that I have back problems, and standing seems to work best for me!"

**"I don't know how it started, either. All I know
is that it's part of our corporate culture."**
www.cartoonbank.com

The fact that employees tend to model and behave like their leaders, which can ultimately translate to results, creates an even more compelling reason for leaders to be aware of the shadow they are casting.

© 1994-2017 Senn Delaney Leadership Consulting Group, LLC. All rights reserved.

managing your shadow

The key to creating and managing the shadow you want is awareness: awareness of the shadow concept and of how the things you say and do influence others. One way to understand the concept is to look at the differences between managing and leading. Managers often attempt to drive their people by prodding and controlling; they are usually behind their people checking results, correcting errors and looking over shoulders. Leaders are usually in front of their people, communicating the vision, illuminating the path and pulling them into action.

There are several reasons why people follow leaders. The first is that we believe the leader will be able to take us somewhere we want to go. We trust our leaders to take us to financial security, opportunities for personal growth and a shared vision. We also look to our leaders for approval, for affirmation that we are on the right track, that our efforts our appreciated.

There is a natural drive to achieve the respect and approval of the important people in our lives. Just as "imitation is the sincerest form of flattery," mimicking the leader's behavior is a natural way of fitting in and achieving approval for our efforts.

As people become aware of their own shadow, they often recognize the shadows that influenced them. One man who found the shadow concept helped him become more effective at work and home gave us the following example:

> "I'm a workaholic and have been for 30 years. I never really thought about having any other choice. It was just the way I was. In fact, all that hard work enabled me to operate much like a machine: a work machine that was unaware of its feelings and emotions.

> "Once I became aware of the shadow concept, I realized that I was just like my father. He would stay up till 1:00 in the morning getting ready for the next day and he'd be out the door by sunrise. I also realized that my daughter, who's a stockbroker, works even harder than I do. Now that I have that realization, I see that I have more choice over how many hours I work, and I can be more of a coach to my kids about their work habits. I feel that it's me causing me to work so hard...not them. I'm not as angry as I used to be and I'm more aware of my feelings. I also listen better to others."

© The New Yorker Collection 1985 Jack Zeigler from cartoonbank.com. All Rights Reserved.

© 1994-2017 Senn Delaney Leadership Consulting Group, LLC. All rights reserved.

Look at your shadow:

- Besides your parents, whose shadow influenced you as you were growing up?
- Whose shadow influenced you early in your career?
- Whose shadow influences you now?
- How have those shadows affected you?
- Whom does your shadow influence?
- How does your shadow affect them?

Managing your shadow is largely a matter of awareness and intent. Here is a simple, three-step process for better understanding your shadow:

Step 1: Identify Your Shadow

What are the elements of your shadow?

Strengths:

_____

_____

Challenges:

_____

_____

Once you have reflected on your shadow and identified your strengths and challenges, ask others in your organization to give you feedback. Talk to your manager, peers and direct reports and get their perception of the shadow you cast. You may even want to get feedback from family and friends. Their perceptions of how you come across in your personal life probably hold some clues to your behavior at work.

You can gain additional insights by looking at the strengths and challenges of the people around you. They often reflect the shadow you cast or the shadow that other leaders in the organization are casting. Review this periodically. As you change, your shadow changes.

Step 2: Develop a Shadow Improvement Plan

Once you have identified areas of possible improvement, look at them closely and determine which ones are most important to you and the people around you. Pick one or two that you feel committed to improve and develop a plan. You may choose to include coaching from someone particularly effective in these areas, or you might find help in a book or class.

Keep in mind that behavior is driven by our thinking. Are there any thought habits that you can identify that might be driving these behaviors?

Behavior(s):

_____

_____

Thought habit(s) that influence this behavior:

_____

_____

senn delaney
the culture-shaping firm

© 1994-2017 Senn Delaney Leadership Consulting Group, LLC. All rights reserved

HEIDRICK & STRUGGLES

Action plan:

_____

_____

Also, tell the people around you what you are doing and ask for feedback. This strengthens your commitment to change, and it also sets up permission for people to provide feedback on your progres.

Step 3: Project Your Shadow

Think of a quality that you would like your organization or team to develop. List several actions or behaviors that would cast that shadow.

Quality/Characteristic:

_____

_____

_____

Specific Action/Behavior:

_____

_____

_____

Put a check (✓) by the actions that come naturally to you and an "X" by the ones that are not part of your normal behavior. What could you do to exhibit the "X" behaviors more frequently?

Although this process is simple, it isn't necessarily easy to execute. It demands a willingness to look closely at your behaviors, to understand your influence on the people around you, and openness to change yourself in order to change the people around you. As the adage says, "If you always do what you've always done, you'll always be what you've always been and always get what you've always gotten."

Mohandas Gandhi said it more eloquently:

> "We must be the change we want to see in the world."

leading the culture: the shadow of the team

The collective shadow cast by an entire organization is called its culture. Successful organizations consciously manage their culture, paying close attention to the examples and values introduced and reinforced by all of management. The high-performance organization shares and lives a distinctive set of norms and values throughout the organization. One of the factors that distinguish the high-performance organization from the standard organization is that the norms and values are lived, preached and practiced wholeheartedly by all of management.

HEIDRICK & STRUGGLES   © 1994-2017 Senn Delaney Leadership Consulting Group, LLC. All rights reserved.

"I want you to nose around and see If anybody's trying to emulate my style."

© The New Yorker Collection 1988 Robert Weber from cartoonbank.com. All Rights Reserved.

Changing an organization's culture begins at the top with senior management, and trickles down through all of management. Whether the organization is a top performer or in drastic need of improvement, change will be resisted, perhaps even sabotaged, until the rest of the organization sees all of management walking the talk. Nothing will happen to the culture if the key leadership team does not live by the values and act as role models.

John D. Macomber, former chairman and president of the Export-Import Bank of the U.S., believes that the ethics of an organization are developed both by leadership and the corporate culture itself. He states:

> "Ethical values are definitely a reflection of leadership. One man or one woman can change the values very quickly. For instance, if an organization senses that it's okay to be a little bit corrupt or dishonest, that value will go through the organization in about ten minutes. But if the people in an organization know that you cannot do wrong and still be an accepted member of that community, they will tend to act ethically. So strong leadership and culture are critical for establishing ethics."[38]

Question: Could others say that you live in integrity by walking your talk and modeling the values you espouse?

influencing the shadow of others

> What happens when a person in the middle of an organization wants to influence the organization's culture? Is it impossible?

The answer is, "Difficult, yes—impossible, no." We are not destined to cast a pre-determined shadow, just because our superiors do. We have a choice. Anyone with broad enough shoulders can choose to cast a healthier shadow themselves than the one they receive from above.

When Gandhi stepped off the boat from England back onto the soil of his homeland India, his shadow was very short. Because he had a powerful vision and all of his behaviors and actions reinforced his message, his shadow grew until it touched the entire world, even though he never held a political office or had any official power.

Besides strengthening our own personal shadow, the other area on which we can focus to build a higher-performing organization is coaching others to cast a healthier shadow. Though many may see this as risky, giving feedback to superiors on the shadow they cast is a significant way of influencing the shadow of your area. This should be done in a way that follows the guidelines for effective coaching discussed earlier.

summary

In Hamlet, Polonius gives the following advice to his son Laertes as he sails for France:

> "This above all: to thine own self be true,
> And it must follow, as the night the day,
> Thou canst not then be false to any man."

We must first look to ourselves in order to manage the impact of behaviors on others, whether at home, in the workplace or in the world at large. By seeing that we walk our talk and keep our agreements, and that we do the most we can to ensure that others will do the same, we do our part to make the world a little better. This is leadership. This is making a difference.

Ask yourself...

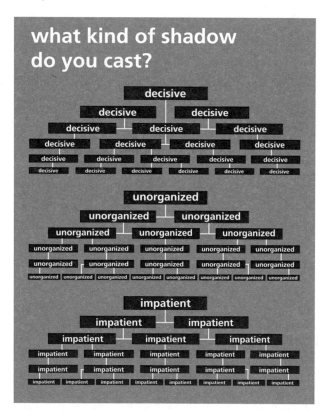

What would you put in the boxes?

HEIDRICK & STRUGGLES

© 1994-2017 Senn Delaney Leadership Consulting Group, LLC. All rights reserved.

questions, action steps and assignments

1. Identify how your shadow affects your organization by listing those things you like in those you influence and those things you dislike. In both columns, check those items that are a shadow of your personal leadership style.

What I Like: What I Dislike:

_____   _____

_____   _____

_____   _____

_____   _____

_____   _____

2. Select one behavior that you would like to see changed in the people you influence or that you would like to see added to their leadership style. Determine how you can initiate this behavior in your organization by role-modeling and casting your shadow. What is your action plan?

Behavior: _____

Action Plan:

_____

_____

_____

_____

_____

3. In addition to your shadow, are there other people whose shadows are having an impact on your area? Which aspects of their shadow are positive and which aspects would you like to see changed? Come up with an action plan for addressing those aspects that you would like to see changed.

Shadow from Others: _____

Action Plan:

_____

_____

_____

_____

© 1994-2017 Senn Delaney Leadership Consulting Group, LLC. All rights reserved.

HEIDRICK & STRUGGLES   © 1994-2017 Senn Delaney Leadership Consulting Group, LLC. All rights reserved.

12

developing a blue-chip mindset

"Don't say you don't have enough time. You have exactly the same number of hours per day that were given to Helen Keller, Pasteur, Michelangelo, Mother Teresa, Leonardo da Vinci, Thomas Jefferson and Albert Einstein."[39]

H. Jackson Brown, Jr.

How often do you hear yourself or others make comments like these:

- I need to create more balance in my life.
- I feel overwhelmed with everything that's on my plate.
- I don't feel like I accomplished enough today.
- Work is on my mind 24/7.

How does one begin to reconcile the need for some balance in life and the need to achieve? How can we add some **Be Here Now** time to our lives and still meet our own standards for accomplishment? There is no easy answer, but it probably isn't by working harder and faster.

Do you remember the poker chip exercise from the unfreezing session? The players from your team, like most, probably worked hard and fast to pick up as many chips as they could. They probably got a good number of chips closest to them, the white chips. The only problem was that the white chips in this game were only worth a dollar apiece, but the less obvious blue chips at the very end of the table were worth $1,000. So for all their hard work, the results weren't as good as they could have been.

The principle is a simple one: execution can be challenging. The first rule of effective time management is to spend your time on the right things. Peter F. Drucker related this to leadership in his book *The Effective Executive*, in which he said, "Time is the scarcest resource, and unless it is managed, nothing else can be managed. The analysis of one's time, moreover, is the one easily accessible and yet systematic way to analyze one's work and think through what really matters in it."[40]

The Blue Chip exercise is a dramatization of a very old principle: Pareto's 80/20 rule, which is, in effect:

> We spend 80% of our time working on things that get us 20% of our results; and the other 20% of our time gets us 80% of our results.

senn delaney
the culture-shaping firm

© 1994-2017 Senn Delaney Leadership Consulting Group, LLC. All rights reserved.

HEIDRICK & STRUGGLES

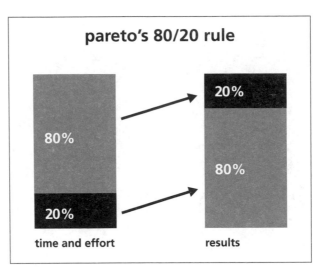

That vitally important 20% is what we call our Blue Chips.

The somewhat important activities that contribute to the accomplishment of goals and objectives, but are not as high-payoff, can often be delegated to someone trustworthy, or handled at your convenience.

The "white chips" are activities that consume a lot of time with very little payoff. They are time-wasters that may not even need to be done, but we do them because we are comfortable doing them, or because they are quick and easy and make us feel like we are getting something done.

The Blue Chip exercise was first created for the field sales force of a Senn Delaney client many years ago. When we were asked to observe their salespeople for ideas on improving performance, we found that they were working even harder than we expected calling on prospects. We also found that they were so busy running from prospect to prospect that they spent little time prioritizing or preparing for the most important prospects.

We helped the client to set up a system to sort out their Blue-Chip prospects, using the Blue Chip game as part of the training. The resulting improvement in sales was dramatic.

At the time, one of the authors of this book was struggling with growing his firm and having time for his growing family. The Blue Chip exercise had such an impact on him that almost every working day since, he has carried a blue poker chip in his pocket; every time he "bumps into it," it raises the question, "Am I focusing my time on the right things?"

personal blue chips

A Blue-Chip mindset applies to our personal lives as much as it does to work. In fact, mastering a Blue-Chip focus at work may help us find time to focus on the other Blue Chips in our lives.

HEIDRICK & STRUGGLES   © 1994-2017 Senn Delaney Leadership Consulting Group, LLC. All rights reserved.

Drawing by P. Kleba; ©1994 SDLCG

It may be easier for us to develop a habit of prioritizing tasks at work. But we should be equally thoughtful of identifying our personal Blue Chips and allocating time to them.

What might be some of your personal Blue Chips?

- Spending quality time with loved ones or friends
- Exercise, fitness or health
- Deepening spiritual understanding
- Contributing to a cause you believe in or the community in which you live
- Refreshing and renewing yourself with a weekend away or a vacation
- Expanding your knowledge or capability through reading or study

Drawing by P. Kleba; ©1994 SDLCG

© 1994-2017 Senn Delaney Leadership Consulting Group, LLC. All rights reserved.

HEIDRICK & STRUGGLES

pointers for making blue-chip thinking a reality

The first step in developing a Blue-Chip mindset is to take a little reflective time to reevaluate your priorities. Start with an initial list of current work and longer-term personal priorities. Keeping a blue poker chip or some other reminder with you can help you keep these at the top of your mind.

In addition, there are a number of things to help ensure you are spending the most time on those things you've identified as being most important to you. The following sections outline these steps:

- Re-examine your thought habits about time use
- Stay focused
- Delegate
- Plan before doing
- Make Blue Chip "to-do" lists

re-examine your thought habits about time use

We all have unconscious habits when it comes to work. Here are a few common ones that can get in our way:

Thinking	Behavior	Results
Important people are always busy.	Spend time on "busy work."	Time is wasted on low-priority activities; low-quality results are produced.
Doing is better than thinking.	Rush into action.	Mistakes or bad decisions; time is wasted on corrective actions.
Thinking is not *working.*	Avoid reflection.	Projects are not properly thought through; time is wasted in stops and starts; problems are not anticipated; opportunities are missed.

Remember, our thinking drives our behaviors, and the quality of our thinking determines when we are at our best.

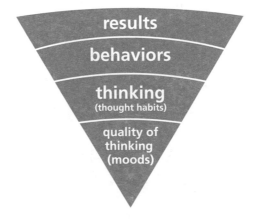

senn delaney
the culture-shaping firm

HEIDRICK & STRUGGLES

© 1994-2017 Senn Delaney Leadership Consulting Group, LLC. All rights reserved.

We are all capable of being brilliant time managers. Poor time management is often a result of being caught up in lower-quality thinking and ineffective thought habits.

Some examples of how higher-quality thinking can influence time management might be:

Thinking	Behavior	Results
It's important to spend time each day identifying my top priorities.	Spend higher percentage of time on projects that yield best results.	High-priority projects are done with top quality; overall results improve.
Delegation helps people grow.	Delegate frequently.	Less important tasks are still accomplished; people grow under my influence.
Planning minimizes execution time.	Spend time planning entire project, creating timelines, identifying possible obstacles, etc.	Projects are completed on time.

Our ability to manage our time effectively fluctuates with the quality of our thinking. The behaviors advocated by typical time management books and articles are good, common-sense habits we naturally exhibit when we are operating in a high-quality thinking state. The problem is, when the quality of our thinking is low, we have limited access to our innate wisdom and common sense and often unconsciously become trapped in less effective thought habits.

Maintaining an awareness of how our thinking affects our performance and gaining an understanding of the key principles of effective time management will help keep us operating effectively even when we are not at our best.

stay focused

When we are clear on our Blue Chips, we tend to stay more focused. When we aren't, we can be pulled in different directions more easily.

Does your day ever seem like the story below?

> A farmer set out one morning to feed his cow. On the way to the barn, he noticed that he had forgotten to put his ax away the night before. He picked up the ax and headed for the tool shed, but on the way he noticed that web worms had gotten into the peach tree. He dropped the ax and went to get paper to burn out the worms.
>
> As he picked up the paper, he remembered an important sale in town and went to his truck. When he opened the garage, he noticed that one of the hinges was loose, so he headed back to the house to get his hammer. On the way to the house, he heard the cow moo so he headed to the barn to feed the cow.
>
> **Question: Did the cow ever get fed?**[41]

© 1994-2017 Senn Delaney Leadership Consulting Group, LLC. All rights reserved.

senn delaney
the culture-shaping firm

HEIDRICK & STRUGGLES

When this begins to happen to you:

- Stop!
- Take a deep breath and regroup;
- Re-think your Blue Chips;
- Then put yourself back in gear.

delegate

Few people have the luxury of only working on Blue Chip items. Most of us are required to keep the flow of lower-priority tasks moving. However, that does not mean that we have to do those tasks ourselves. If we want to be high performers, and spend more of our time focusing on the Blue Chips, we need to effectively utilize our team. One of the key skills of a successful team leader is mastering the art of delegation. Delegation is critical because it not only helps you to be more effective, it develops the skills of your team members, increasing their effectiveness as well.

Theodore Roosevelt once said:

> "The best executive is one who has sense enough to pick good people to do what should be done and self-restraint enough to keep from meddling with them while they do it."[42]

It makes little sense to assemble a high-quality team and then not give them the authority and responsibility to do what needs to be done. The successful team leader makes sure the team sees the vision, understands what needs to be done, and has the tools and knowledge necessary to do it.

Many leaders find delegation difficult. Some find it hard to let go and trust others to accomplish an important task. Others are afraid to look like they are "dumping" their work on others. Here are several typical thought habits that create internal barriers to delegation:

- **Ego:** I can do it better myself.
- **Lack of patience:** I don't have time to show them how to do it.
- **Lack of trust:** I don't know if they will do it well enough.
- **Comfort:** I like to do this task.
- **Lack of confidence in coaching skills:** I don't know how to teach them to do it.
- **Fear of burdening others:** It's my job; I should do it.

What might be some of your barriers?

The key to effective delegation is delegating the right task to the right person. This person should:

- Understand your vision and desired outcomes.
- Be qualified and willing to perform the task.
- Be willing to be accountable for results.
- Have the authority to carry out actions.
- Feel trusted to achieve the desired results.

HEIDRICK & STRUGGLES

© 1994-2017 Senn Delaney Leadership Consulting Group, LLC. All rights reserved.

It is important that you and the person to whom you delegate have an understanding of the above issues, and a relationship of trust; you need to have faith in the person to do the job you've given them, and the person needs to know that they can come to you if they need assistance or input.

However, trust does not mean that you need to let go completely. If the task is your ultimate responsibility, it is still incumbent on you to make sure it is done. It may be helpful to establish ground rules at the beginning of the process, such as when and how often you'd like to check in with the person to monitor their progress, and whether or not you need to review the final result. As you and your people become more comfortable with the delegation process, you will find the need to check in and review will decrease over time.

Plan Before Doing

In our busy, often chaotic world, planning is sometimes pushed aside in the rush to put out today's fires. People frequently complain that they are too busy to plan their time, yet statistics show that planning actually reduces overall time spent accomplishing any goal.

It is almost paradoxical that we have so little time that we cannot devote even part of it to the one thing that will give us more time: planning!

Make Blue Chip "To-Do" Lists

High achievers tend to focus on their Blue Chips by preparing a daily "to do" list, prioritizing the tasks in terms of how close each one will bring them to their Blue Chip goals, and then following the plan, focusing on the highest-return activities first.

Try organizing your to-do list by Blue Chip and white chip categories.

summary

At the beginning of this chapter, we referred to several people who are well known for their great accomplishments. One reason these people were so effective was that they were willing to devote time to determining what was really important to them.

Getting the most from life requires the same from each of us: to take the time to achieve a clear understanding of what is important. Because our state of mind affects the choices we make from moment to moment, this understanding gives us a tool to choose activities—the Blue Chips—that will take us to our goals and objectives, even when we're not thinking clearly. Remembering to take the time to plan, exhibiting the discipline to execute and the being willing to delegate are additional tools to help us stay on track, on time and on target to reach the goals that mean the most in our lives.

© 1994-2017 Senn Delaney Leadership Consulting Group, LLC. All rights reserved.

senn delaney
the culture-shaping firm

HEIDRICK & STRUGGLES

questions, action steps and assignments

1. What are your current work-related Blue Chips?

   _____

   _____

   _____

2. What are or should be your personal Blue Chips?

   _____

   _____

   _____

3. What pointers or ideas from this chapter will you commit to use to focus better on the items listed above?

   _____

   _____

senn delaney
the culture-shaping firm

HEIDRICK & STRUGGLES

© 1994-2017 Senn Delaney Leadership Consulting Group, LLC. All rights reserved.

13

making change
a way of life

We hope your unfreezing experience inspired you. We also hope you had some insights into how you can achieve even more results and fulfillment in your life.

Many people ask us, "What can I do to make the changes a way of life?" If that is a desire of yours, then you have some accountability in making that happen. The culture-shaping session is designed to create insights and commitments, or "I will…" statements. Long-term benefits require that you find ways to reinforce what you learned and apply the behaviors in your daily life.

Reading and re-reading this book is part of that reinforcement. Keeping your pocket contract card, Blue Chip, Be Here Now plaque or other such reminders visible is another way to reinforce those concepts. Hopefully, you are also on our eCoach® online reinforcement system as well. When those messages arrive, find a few quiet moments to view those brief reminders and apply the tips they give you.

Application is largely in your hands. The old saying, "use it or lose it" applies not only to fitness and our bodies, but to new, healthy habits and commitments. Application begins with becoming more aware of your thinking and/or approach to day-to-day situations. Here are some questions to ask yourself and discuss with others as these situations arise:

human operating system

- Whenever I find myself too certain or self-righteous it may be a good time to remember the F's and ask, "What am I missing?"
- When I feel judgmental, can I at least move up the Mood Elevator to curious?
- What are my personal filters, and how do they affect the way I approach people, meetings and challenging situations?
- What thought habits might be getting in the way of my understanding in this situation?
- How is the quality of my thinking or mood affecting my behavior right now?
- Is this a good time for me to make this decision, given where I am on the Mood Elevator?

senn delaney
the culture-shaping firm

HEIDRICK & STRUGGLES

© 1994-2017 Senn Delaney Leadership Consulting Group, LLC. All rights reserved.

be here now

- Am I Being Here Now?
- At what level am I listening to this person?
- Am I able to listen for understanding right now, or should I delay this conversation until I'm better able to put aside distractions?

at your best

- What's my "unhealthy normal?"
- When "it's all about me," I should beware, because my thinking is unreliable.
- When my thinking becomes circular, maybe I need a pattern interrupt to clear my mind.

behavioral styles

- What's the best way to work with that style?
- What are some ways I can flex my style to be more effective with this person?

coaching

- Do I give my family and employees/co-workers enough appreciative feedback?
- What coaching opportunities am I missing with others?
- Am I in the right mood state to coach now or should I wait?
- Am I talking too much or listening enough as a coach?

blue-chip mindset

- What are my Blue Chips in life and in my job?
- Can I delegate this task to another?
- Do I even need to spend my time on this white chip?
- How does this activity fit in with my life priorities?
- How will this activity help me achieve my goals?

accountability

- What more can I do?
- Is blaming others or feeling victimized getting in the way of a better outcome in this situation? How might I think and behave differently to get better results?
- Is this something I/we can influence, or is this a gravity issue?
- Am I living the Serenity Prayer?

teamwork

- Am I using the wisdom of the team?
- Am I too focused on my own square?
- How big of a team am I willing to play on?
- Am I playing win-win or win-lose with teammates?

senn delaney
the culture-shaping firm

HEIDRICK & STRUGGLES

© 1994-2017 Senn Delaney Leadership Consulting Group, LLC. All rights reserved.

change

- Is my first reaction to new ideas as a participant/supporter/coach? Or an observer/critic/judge?
- Am I treating new ideas like the unconventional wheelbarrow?

shadow of the leader

- What shadow am I casting now?
- Do I role-model the values and behaviors I espouse?
- How can I use my shadow to influence positive results?

By consistently reminding yourself of these tips, you keep the concepts alive until they become positive habits.

The essence of application is "walking the talk," or living the Essential Values as best you can. This means:

- Being accountable, not a victim
- Being a collaborative team player
- Being flexible and open to change, not an observer/critic/judge
- Being a coach and not a "boss"
- Contributing to team and organizational health by striving to:
  - Be Here Now and listen
  - Live "up the Mood Elevator" and be cautious when you're down
  - Be respectful of all styles and people

Will you be able to do all of this all of the time? Of course not. Should you beat yourself up when you don't? No! (That only takes you down the Mood Elevator.)

Just practice being more aware and conscious of how you are doing and you will naturally begin to do better. Asking others for feedback on how you're doing is a great way to become more aware.

two parting thoughts

1. You already "walk the talk" when you are "up on the Mood Elevator" and at your best.

So if there is one Blue Chip to focus on, it is living more of life at your best and knowing when you're not, so you can adjust.

2. Life, like leadership, is a journey, not a destination.

Just stay on the path and try to stay pointed in the right direction.

Best of luck on your journey!

© 1994-2017 Senn Delaney Leadership Consulting Group, LLC. All rights reserved.

about Senn Delaney

Senn Delaney was founded in 1978 with a singular mission: to create healthy, high-performance cultures. We were the first firm in the world to focus exclusively on transforming organizational cultures. More Fortune 500 and Global 1000 CEOs have chosen us as their trusted partner to help shape cultures that deliver better business results.

Our work is focused on improving performance in a variety of business situations. The most common drivers of our work include:

Aligning new leaders and/or newly configured teams

- Maximize effectiveness of the team more quickly
- Prepare them to best lead culture change

Avoiding cultural clash in mergers and acquisitions

- Avoid, smooth or pre-empt the culture clashes that often keep mergers and acquisitions from realizing full potential and synergy

Shaping the culture to support new strategies

- Determine habits that may slow progress of new strategies
- Develop and align entire company around new values and guiding behaviors

Supporting change in major organization-wide systems or processes

- Minimize cultural barriers to change

Gaining cross-organizational synergies from a shared business model

- Create collaborative organizations to effectively implement shared services and allied business models
- Gain cross-organizational synergies

Creating a more customer-focused organization with improved customer satisfaction

- Create service cultures to support company-wide efficiency and performance and enable top-line growth

Our passion and singular focus on culture, combined with decades of hands-on experience, has resulted in a comprehensive and proven culture-shaping methodology that engages people and measurably impacts both the spirit and performance of organizations. Our process includes connecting clients with the principles and values outlined in this book. The process generally begins with the CEO and senior team and is carried throughout an organization from top to bottom.

We are an international culture-shaping firm with offices in California, New York and London. To best serve our clients around the world, our partners and consultants are located throughout the US, the UK, and Europe. We have delivered our work in more than 40 countries and many of our culture-shaping tools are offered in a dozen languages.

HEIDRICK & STRUGGLES

© 1994-2017 Senn Delaney Leadership Consulting Group, LLC. All rights reserved.

On Dec. 31, 2012, we began an exciting new chapter in our long history when we were acquired by Heidrick & Struggles International, Inc., the premier provider of executive search and leadership consulting services worldwide. All of the Senn Delaney partners, consultants and staff are committed to maintaining our unique, healthy culture by living our values. This commitment to our values and the engaging and authentic way in which we show up not only produces better business results, but it makes working with us a positive and enriching experience for our clients.

On Dec. 31, 2012, we began an exciting new chapter in our long history when we were acquired by Heidrick & Struggles International, Inc., the premier provider of executive search and leadership consulting services worldwide.

To learn more, visit our Web site, www.senndelaney.com or contact us at:

Senn Delaney
7755 Center Avenue, Suite 900
Huntington Beach, CA 92647
t (562) 426-5400
f (562) 426-5174

info@senndelaney.com

© 1994-2017 Senn Delaney Leadership Consulting Group, LLC. All rights reserved.

about the principal authors

Larry Senn is a pioneer in the area of high-performance teams and cultures. His USC doctoral dissertation, *Organization Character*, published in 1969, was the first field study of corporate culture in America. Since its formation in 1978, Senn Delaney has become the most experienced and successful culture-shaping firm in the world. Larry has led teams that have re-shaped cultures of major firms in the telecommunications, energy, banking, retailing, manufacturing and consumer products industries. He has also worked with governors of states, members of U.S. President's cabinets, presidents of major universities and deans of business schools.

Bernadette Senn contributed many of the concepts and much of the content in the book. She helped pioneer the learning technology used by Senn Delaney in its culture-shaping work, primarily with retail clients in the 1970s and 80s. A graduate of the University of Southern California's MBA program in Organizational Behavior, Bernadette developed much of the seminar content used by the firm, as well as the process to train both Senn Delaney facilitators and client facilitators of the core unfreezing session, which is key element in the overall culture-shaping process.

As in all the work we do, this book was a team effort. There were a lot of people behind the scenes at Senn Delaney that made it possible. They included Celeste Rothstein who managed the book project; Paul Diniakos who created the cover, the graphics and the layout of the book; Darin Senn and Kathleen Tomaino who provided consultant field input; Margee Infante and Judy Gesicki for typing and proofing.

HEIDRICK & STRUGGLES

© 1994-2017 Senn Delaney Leadership Consulting Group, LLC. All rights reserved.

X

attributions

text notes

Human Operating System

1. Thomas J. Peters and Robert H. Waterman, *In Search of Excellence* (New York: Harper & Row, 1982)

2. Jill Bolte Taylor, PhD., *My Stroke of Insight* (New York: Penguin Group, 2006) p. 139

3. *My Stroke of Insight*, p. 142

4. *My Stroke of Insight*, p. 142

Be Here Now

5. S.I. Hayakawa, *Symbol, Status and Personality* (New York: Harcourt, Brace & World, 1953)

6. *Humor, Risk and Change*™ (Prod. American Media, Inc.)

At Your Best

7. Daniel Goleman, *Emotional Intelligence: Why It Can Matter More than IQ* (New York: Bantam, 1995), p. 92

8. Gary W. Evans, Peter Lercher, Markus Meis et.al, "Community Noise Exposure and Stress in Children," *Journal of the Acoustical Society of America* (Vol. 109, March 2001)

9. Jim Loehr, and Tony Schwartz, *The Power of Full Engagement: Managing Energy, Not Time, is the Key to High Performance and Personal Renewal* (New York: Free Press, a division of Simon and Schuster, Inc. 2003), p. 29

10. *The Power of Full Engagement: Managing Energy, Not Time, is the Key to High Performance and Personal Renewal*, p. 44

11. Deborah Norville, *Thank You Power: Making the Science of Gratitude Work for You* (Nashville: Thomas Nelson, Inc., 2007), p. 22

© 1994-2017 Senn Delaney Leadership Consulting Group, LLC. All rights reserved.

Essential Values

12. Tom Peters, *A Passion for Excellence* (New York: Random House, 1985), p. XXV

13. Michael Lynburg, *Winning* (New York: Doubleday, 1993), p. 31

14. Henry Erlich, *The Wiley Book of Business Quotations* (New York: John Wiley & Sons, Inc. 1998). p. 88

15. Kenneth Blanchard and Norman Vincent Peale, *The Power of Ethical Management* (New York: Fawcett Crest, 1988)

Building a Winning Culture

16. Tony Athos and Richard Tanner Pascale, *The Art of Japanese Management* (New York: Warner Books Inc., 1982)

17. John P. Kotter, *Corporate Culture and Performance* (New York: Free Press, a division of Simon and Schuster, 1992)

18. Lynn Joy McFarland, Larry E. Senn, and John R. Childress, *21st Century Leadership: Dialogues with 100 Top Leaders* (Los Angeles: The Leadership Press, 1993), p. 162

Accountability

19. Georgette Mosbacher, *Feminine Force* (New York: Simon & Schuster, 1993), p. 285

20. *21st Century Leadership*, p. 80

21. Charles J. Sykes, *A Nation of Victims* (New York: St. Martin's Press, 1992), p. 13, 253

Teamwork

22. Robert Reich, "Entrepreneurship Reconsidered: the Team as Hero," *The Harvard Business Review*, May-June 1987

23. Jon R. Katzenbach and Douglas K. Smith, *The Wisdom of Teams*, (Massachusetts: Harvard Business School Press, 1993) p. 15

24. *21st Century Leadership*, p. 56

25. "Entrepreneurship Reconsidered: the Team as Hero"

26. *The Wisdom of Teams*, p. 15

27. Dr. Robert McNeish, former Associate Superintendent of Baltimore Public Schools; written for a lay sermon at Northminster Presbyterian Church, 1972; transcribed from a speech given by Angeles Arrrien at the 1991 Organizational Development Network. (http://sue-widemark.com/lessonsgeese.htm)

Change

28. *21st Century Leadership*, p. 219

29. Sandra Lotz Fisher, "Warning Signs and Identifying Characteristics; Stress, Part 1," *Sales & Marketing Management*, Nov. 1992, p. 93

30. "Warning Signs and Identifying Characteristics; Stress, Part 1"

31. Todd D. Jick, "Managing Change" in *The Portable MBA in Management*, Ed. Allen R. Cohen (Toronto: John Wiley & Sons, Inc., 1993), p. 367

Coaching and Feedback

32. Lawrence J. Bradford and Claire Raines, *Twentysomething* (New York: Master Media Limited, 1992), p. 24-29

Shadow of the Leader

33. Larry E. Senn and John R. Childress, *Secret of a Winning Culture* (Los Angeles: Leadership Press, 1999), p. 82

34. Dorothy Law Nolte, "Children Learn What They Live" (Ross Laboratories, *Living Scrolls*, 1972)

35. Shelley A. Kirkpatrick and Edwin A. Locke, "Leadership: Do Traits Matter?" *Academy of Management Executive*, May 1991, p. 57

36. Carole King, "Leading the Field by Example, Not the Rulebook," *The National Underwriter*, Sept. 1991, p. 31

37. *21st Century Leadership*, p. 151

38. *21st Century Leadership*, p. 125

Developing a Blue-Chip Mindset

39. H. Jackson Brown, Jr., *Life's Little Instruction Book* (Nashville TN: Rutledge Hill Press, 1991)

40. Peter F. Drucker, *The Effective Executive* (New York: HarperCollins, 1967), p. 51

41. Alec Mackenzie, *The Time Trap* (New York: AMACOM, 1972)

42. Louise E. Boone, *Quotable Business* (New York: Random House, Inc. 1992), p. 19

© 1994-2017 Senn Delaney Leadership Consulting Group, LLC. All rights reserved.

senn delaney
the culture-shaping firm

HEIDRICK & STRUGGLES

HEIDRICK & STRUGGLES

© 1994-2017 Senn Delaney Leadership Consulting Group, LLC. All rights reserved.